NATIONAL GEOGRAPHIC KIDS

ULTIMATE Explorer
FIELD GUIDE

Trees

Patricia Daniels

NATIONAL GEOGRAPHIC
WASHINGTON, D.C.

RED MANGROVE,
PAGE 61

Contents

**CRAPE MYRTLE,
PAGE 75**

**TASMANIAN
BLUEGUM,
PAGE 102**

LET'S LOOK AT TREES

AUTUMN LEAVES
IN VERMONT

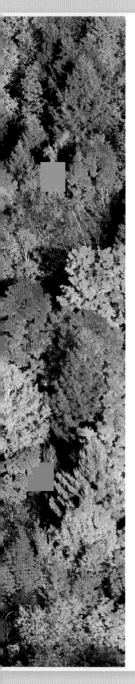

CONGRATULATIONS ON YOUR ADVENTURE INTO THE TREES!

There are many ways to know the trees around us, and in *National Geographic Kids Ultimate Explorer Field Guide: Trees,* you will find out how—as you meet both eastern and western trees. You will learn that some trees prefer cool climates and some prefer heat. Others may have different moisture, sunlight, and soil needs.

When you look at trees, keep in mind that they make important contributions to the health of our planet. Trees reduce erosion, so they help keep soil out of streams and rivers. Trees clean our air and help keep temperatures from climbing too high or dropping too low. They absorb and store carbon dioxide and provide oxygen. Forest health is critical to addressing climate change.

That's why trees need our protection, too. Trees face challenges today. They are cut down to provide land for roads, housing, and other uses. Additionally, insects and diseases are threatening some species. Warmer air temperatures and drought challenge trees that may have been able to fight off insects and disease in past years. In many areas of North America, the overpopulation of deer is harming forests, as they nibble at young shoots, keeping them from growing into full-size trees.

The distinct personalities of different trees are tied to their individual evolution and adapation to their environment. Native trees are descendants of trees that were here before European explorers and settlers came to North America. They have evolved with our native insects, birds, and other animals. Other trees, non-native or exotic, have been brought here from other continents and will have a different relationship with other players in the environment. We have to watch them carefully so that they do not take over the native plants that play an important part in the North American ecosystem.

We hope that *National Geographic Kids Ultimate Explorer Field Guide: Trees* will inspire you to enjoy and protect our trees and that you'll have fun doing it!

—Tony Dove and Ginger Woolridge,
authors, *Essential Native Trees and Shrubs
for the Eastern United States*

HOW TO USE This Book

LOOK AROUND! You may see trees as tall as two-story buildings or as short as bushes, or you may not see trees at all until you go to a local park. Wherever you find trees, use this guide to learn about them!

Cuban Royal Palm Page 143

Tree Entry

THIS IS WHERE YOU'LL FIND THE TREE'S COMMON NAME.

HERE IS THE TREE'S SCIENTIFIC NAME, ITS ORDER, ITS AVERAGE HEIGHT, THE ENVIRONMENT IT LIVES IN, AND WHERE IT GROWS IN NORTH AMERICA.

White Oak

Quercus alba HEIGHT 50–80 ft (15–24.5 m) · SHAPE **Medium to tall, with wide, irregular crown** · LEAVES **Alternate, simple, 5–7 in (12.5–18 cm), deeply lobed, with smooth, rounded edges** · FLOWERS **Hanging green catkins** · FRUITS **Acorns** · RANGE **Eastern United States** · HABITAT **Widespread in woods and yards** · OTHER NAME **Eastern White Oak**

THIS TEXT GIVES GENERAL INFORMATION ABOUT THE SPECIES, INCLUDING BARK AND LEAVES TO LOOK FOR AND SOME COOL, SURPRISING FACTS.

If you live in the eastern United States, you've probably seen plenty of White Oaks. These tall and wide-spreading trees with shaggy gray bark are among the most common trees in the country. White Oaks are prized for their wood, which is often used for floors and woodwork in houses. Animals such as squirrels and blue jays like them for their tasty acorns, which ripen at the end of one season, which lasts a year. Creatures snatch them from the ground and store them in hiding places. White Oaks can live up to 600 years and grow as tall as 100 feet (30.5 m).

→ LOOK FOR THIS
Most oaks are divided into two groups: **RED OAKS** and **WHITE OAKS**. Red oaks have reddish wood, and white oak wood is creamy white.

Red oaks have the following:
- Leaves with pointed lobes and sharp bristles on their tips
- Flat scales on the acorn cup
- Dark, smooth, or ridged bark

White oaks have the following:
- Leaves usually with rounded, smooth lobes
- Bumpy scales on the acorn cup
- Paler, scaly bark

DISCOVER FUN FACTS OR IDENTIFYING TIPS FROM EXPERTS ABOUT EACH SPECIES.

IDENTIFY A TREE BY LOOKING FOR THESE BASIC FEATURES. CAN YOU NAME THE CORRECT SPECIES IN 10 SECONDS?

CLASSIFICATION TAB

CUP COVERS ONE-THIRD OF LIGHT BROWN ACORN.

LEAVES WITH MEDIUM TO DEEP LOBES; SMOOTH ROUNDED EDGES.

SPECIAL FEATURES CALLED TREE-MENDOUS give you a closer look at trees' appearance, their amazing growth patterns, and their remarkable flowers and leaves.

A CAPTION
DESCRIBES
THE MAIN
PHOTO.

A TEXT BLOCK GIVES GENERAL INFORMATION
ABOUT THE SPECIAL FEATURES OF APPEARANCE,
SEASONAL CYCLES, OR CONSERVATION.

LEARN ABOUT THE DIFFERENT
SPECIES THAT REPRESENT THE
THEME OF TREE-MENDOUS.

Classification

TREES HAVE BOTH COMMON NAMES AND SCIENTIFIC NAMES. Common names are the ones you usually know, such as Red Maple or Weeping Willow. It's good to know common names, but you'll find that they can be confusing. One tree can have many common names, and some of them might make you think it is a different kind of tree. For instance, the Eastern Redcedar is not a cedar, but a juniper tree.

Scientific names are more precise. Each tree has only one scientific name, which is in Latin and has two parts: genus and species. The genus name is capitalized and is the tree's immediate group. For instance, all oak trees are in the genus *Quercus*. The species name identifies one particular kind of tree within a genus. For instance, the species name for the Pin Oak is *palustris*. So the scientific name for Pin Oak is *Quercus palustris*.

Each tree belongs to a bigger family, the family is part of an even bigger order, and the order is part of a very big group. Finally, all trees are in the kingdom of plants. Here's how the Pin Oak fits in:

Kingdom: Plantae (plants)

Group: Angiospermae (all flowering plants)

Order: Fagales (a kind of flowering plant)

Family: Fagaceae (Beech tree)

Genus: *Quercus*

Species: *palustris*

WHAT IS A Tree?

IF THERE WERE A PRIZE FOR THE GREATEST PLANT ON EARTH, the tree would be a top contender. Trees are the tallest and oldest living things on our planet. Trees give us, and other animals, shade and shelter. They take carbon out of the air and put oxygen into the air so we can breathe. They help keep water clean, and they cool our homes and streets in the summer. And they are beautiful, with their shining leaves, their colorful flowers, and their curving branches. But what is a tree, exactly?

Trees are different from other plants because they have upright woody stems called trunks. The U.S. Forest Service defines a tree as a woody plant that is usually large and will grow to at least 15 feet (4.5 m) tall with a trunk at least three inches (7.5 cm) around. It also has a definite crown—the part near the top of the tree filled with leafy branches. Smaller woody plants are called shrubs. There's not a big difference between a tall shrub and a multistemmed short tree.

THE PARTS OF A TREE

Let's look at a typical tree from the ground up:

GIANT SEQUOIA, PAGE 21

Trunks

TRUNKS Trunks are what make trees, trees. Tree trunks have two main uses. They hold up leaves, and they carry water up and food down the tree. Trunks are covered with a tough bark, which protects the tree. The spongy inner layer of bark, the phloem, carries food downward to feed all parts of the tree, including the roots. Under the phloem is the cambium layer. This is the part of the trunk that grows, making new bark on the outside and new wood on the inside. Under the cambium are two layers of the wood itself, sapwood (also called xylem) and heartwood.

Sapwood is young wood that carries water. Inside this, at the center of the tree, is heartwood, made of sapwood cells that have died. Heartwood is strong and supports the tree.

Roots

ROOTS Tree roots spread out shallowly under the soil until they are about as wide as the tree's leafy crown. They pull water and essential minerals out of the soil for use by the tree. They also hold the tree in the ground so it doesn't fall over!

EASTERN WHITE PINE, PAGE 46

CALIFORNIA SYCAMORE,
PAGE 105

Branches

BRANCHES Woody branches grow out of the main trunk to hold leaves out into the light. Bigger branches might lead to smaller, younger branchlets. At the end of the branches or branchlets are young twigs. Twigs start growing in the spring. In the summer, they make buds, which will give birth to new leaves and flowers the next spring. A tree's crown is all the branches and leaves together—the green spreading part of the tree.

LEAVES Leaves are usually flat and green, although in coni-fer trees they may be sharp and pointy, like needles. They attach to a twig on a short stalk called a petiole. Leaves are a tree's food factories. Through a process called photosynthesis, they pull a gas called carbon dioxide from the air, add water and sunlight, and turn it into sugar and a gas called oxygen. The tree eats the sugar, and the oxygen goes into the air. The best way to identify a tree is through its leaves, as you'll see in the following pages.

Leaves

JAPANESE MAPLE, PAGE 54

FLOWERS AND SEEDS Many trees produce flowers in the spring, although they may be so small that you don't notice them. All trees make seeds, which are covered by cones or fruits (read more about them on pages 12–13).

Flowers and seeds

SWEET CRABAPPLE, PAGE 111

TREES WITH Flowers, TREES WITH Cones

THE TREES IN THIS BOOK BELONG TO TWO BIG GROUPS AND A THIRD TINY GROUP.

CONIFERS

Trees that have cones, but not true flowers or fruits, are known as conifers. They belong to the larger group of plants called gymnosperms. ("Gymnosperm" means "naked seed.") Their seeds are tucked into tough cones or little berrylike cups.

Conifer leaves look like sharp needles or scales. We often call conifers "evergreens" because most of them keep their leaves through the winter. However, a few conifers, such as the Baldcypress (see page 24), do change color and drop their leaves in the fall. Those evergreens aren't ever-green! Some well-known conifers:

Conifer

✓ Cypresses
✓ Pines
✓ Firs
✓ Junipers
✓ Spruces

**ENGELMANN SPRUCE
WITH CONIFERS,
PAGE 33**

BROADLEAF TREES

Broadleaf

Broadleaf trees have broader, flatter leaves than conifers. In the springtime, they grow flowers. Seeds grow from the flowers and are sheltered inside a closed fruit. When we think of fruit, we think of apples or pears. But little maple wings or tough shells such as walnuts are also considered fruits, protecting the seeds inside. Broadleaf trees are part of a larger group of plants known as angiosperms (which means "vessel seeds").

**SUGAR MAPLE
AND ITS SAMARAS,
PAGE 56**

PECAN NUT, PAGE 138

Most broadleaf trees are deciduous in climates with cold winters. That means they drop their leaves in the fall as the weather cools, and they grow new ones in the spring when it warms up. However, some like to hang on to their leaves even in cold weather. Look around in winter and you'll see some oaks, beeches, or other trees stubbornly holding on to brown leaves. Those leaves will fall off in the spring when the tree grows new buds.

There are many kinds of flowering trees. Some well-known ones include:

- ✓ Maples
- ✓ Oaks
- ✓ Willows
- ✓ Birches
- ✓ Elms
- ✓ Hickories
- ✓ Palms

GINKGOES

The third main group of trees has only one member: the Ginkgo. The Ginkgo is neither a conifer nor a flowering tree; instead, it belongs to its own division of plants. You can read more about the weird, prehistoric Ginkgo on pages 50–51.

Ginkgo

GINKGO LEAVES, PAGE 50

KNOW YOUR Leaves

ALL LEAVES DO THE SAME THING: They make sugar to feed the tree. But leaves come in many different shapes and sizes. Each tree has its own special leaf shape. That's why leaves are one of the main things you look at when you're trying to identify a tree.

Leaves can be grouped by their shapes and how they line up on a twig. Here are some of the most common shapes.

CONIFER LEAVES

Needles. Sharp, pointed leaves that spray out from one bud **1** or line up along the twig or branchlet **2**

Scales. Flat, small leaves that wrap tightly around the twig **3**

BROAD LEAVES

Simple. Single, flat leaves. Some have smooth edges; others are toothed, like the cutting edge of a saw. Some have lobes: Their edges go in and out, like a duck's webbed foot.

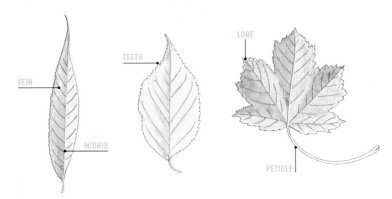

Compound. Many small leaflets sticking out from each side of a central stalk that grows out of a branch. A leaf is attached to the central stalk by a smaller stalk called a petiole.

LEAF ARRANGEMENTS

Leaves can line up in two ways on a branch or twig.
Opposite. Two or three leaves grow facing each other from the same spot on the twig.
Alternate. Leaves grow from different spots, alternating along the twig.

JAPANESE MAPLE,
PAGE 54

GETTING STARTED

ARE YOU READY TO NAME THAT TREE? Take this book with you and follow a few simple rules.

DOS AND DON'TS

When you're out for a tree walk, stay safe and be smart. For instance:

Do take a trusted adult with you whenever you go out to explore.

Do go out in summer or early fall. That's when leaves are fully grown. It's harder (but not impossible!) to identify a tree in winter.

Do dress for a hike. If you're walking through fields or woods, wear long pants, socks, and closed-toe shoes. That way, insects won't bite your legs and thorns won't scratch your skin.

Do watch out for critters. Trees are home to insects and other creatures. Keep your eyes open for animals that might bite or sting. And always leave animals alone.

POISON IVY, PAGE 53

Don't touch any plant with three leaves. Poison ivy can grow on the ground or up the trunk of a tree as a vine. If you rub it, it can give you a terrible, itchy rash. Know what it looks like, and remember: *Leaves of three, let it be.*

Don't hurt your fine green friends, the trees. Don't break live tree branches or cut into or peel off tree bark.

Don't lick or eat seeds, bark, or leaves. Some trees, like the Pacific Yew (see page 49), have highly poisonous parts.

Don't collect any leaves unless you have the permission of the tree's owner.

Don't take leaves or anything else if you're in a protected area, like a national park.

EASTERN HEMLOCK,
PAGE 48

START WITH LEAVES

To start identifying a tree, begin with its leaves. Are they needlelike or scaly? Are they broad and flat? Note whether the leaves have smooth or toothed edges. Are they lobed, like a hand? Do the tree's twigs hold single leaves, or little leaflets along a single stalk? Are the leaves opposite each other, or do they alternate on the twig? Find the trees with those sorts of leaves in the guidebook.

OTHER THINGS TO LOOK FOR

- **Shape.** Is the tree's crown (the leafy part) round, pointy, or conical (cone-shaped)? Be aware that two trees of the same species can have different shapes. It depends on how crowded they are, how much sun they get, and how old they are.

- **Flowers or cones.** Can you see flowers on the tree? What do they look like? How about cones? What are their shape and size?

PACIFIC
DOGWOOD,
PAGE 60

- **Fruit.** Does the tree have little winged seeds, acorns, or other growths that look like nuts or berries?

- **Bark.** Is it smooth or rough? What color is it? Is it peeling off?

- **Habitat.** Check the tree's surroundings. Are they wet and marshy? Open and sunny? Hills or valleys?

NAME THAT TREE!

You've spotted two different trees in a nearby forest. Try to name them by finding the matching entry on the following pages of this guide.

Tree #1: This tree is tall! It has widely spaced branches. Its blue-green needles grow in bunches of five, and its brown cones are long and scraggly.

Tree #2: This tree has a short trunk and a wide, leafy crown. Its leaves grow across from each other on their stems. They have five deep, pointy lobes, green on top and silvery underneath. Long, winglike seeds in pairs drop from its branches.

2. Silver Maple (page 55)
1. Eastern White Pine (page 46)

Alaska Cedar

Chamaecyparis nootkatensis HEIGHT 50–125 ft (15–38 m)
· SHAPE Cone-shaped · LEAVES Scales · CONES Round, scaly
· RANGE Southeastern Alaska to Northern California · HABITAT
Mountains · OTHER NAMES Yellow Cypress, Nootka Cypress,
Nootka False Cypress

One of the few West Coast trees that can also grow well on the East Coast, the slow-growing Alaska Cedar loves the snow and can live to be thousands of years old. Pale and silvery, its bark peels in strips from a reddish layer underneath. Alaska Cedar leaves are tightly packed scales that cover the tree's branchlets. You definitely don't want to touch these leaves—squeezing them gives off a nasty, oily smell.

→ LOOK FOR THIS

The green, scaly branchlets of the **ALASKA CEDAR** hang down from the main branches like shaggy curtains.

TINY, SCALELIKE
LEAVES

ROUND CONES WITH
POINTY SCALES

HANGING
BRANCHLETS

Junipers give food and shelter to all kinds of animals. Birds eat the cones, and mammals such as white-tailed deer find cover under their sweet-smelling branches. Cooks use the cones in sauces and drinks.

Atlantic White Cedar

Chamaecyparis thyoides HEIGHT 50–80 ft (15–24.5 m)
· SHAPE **Narrow, pointed** · LEAVES **Scales** · CONES **Round, scaly**
· RANGE **Maine to Florida to Mississippi** · HABITAT **Swamps, wet sands**
· OTHER NAMES **Southern White Cedar, Swamp Cedar**

This spicy-smelling conifer grows well in wet places such as swamps and bogs. Its wood is light and strong and doesn't decay easily. That's why, for centuries, people have been cutting down Atlantic White Cedars to build ships, barrels, and telephone poles. For this reason—and because their habitat is often cleared for buildings—it's hard to find many big, old Atlantic White Cedars anymore.

Eastern Redcedar

Juniperus virginiana HEIGHT 30–60 ft (9–18.5 m) · SHAPE **Cone-shaped**
· LEAVES **Scales** · CONES **Round, blue or purple, berrylike** · RANGE **Eastern United States, from southeastern Canada to the Gulf of Mexico** · HABITAT **Open fields, roadsides, fence rows** · OTHER NAMES **Red Juniper, Pencil Cedar**

The Eastern Redcedar is not actually a cedar, but a juniper tree. Like all junipers, its cones don't look like cones at all, but more like berries. You'll see this medium-size conifer growing all over the eastern United States along roads and in empty pastures. Eastern Redcedars can have two kinds of leaves on one tree. The young ones are needles and the older ones are scaly. The tree's reddish brown bark peels off in thin strips, and its pleasant-smelling wood is often used to line closets and drawers. Birds like to eat the berries, and by carrying the seeds around they help spread the trees far and wide.

Redwood

Sequoia sempervirens HEIGHT **200–325 ft (61–99 m)** · SHAPE **Tall, slender, cone-shaped** · LEAVES **1-in (2.5-cm) needles** · CONES **Small, brown, scaly** · RANGE **Pacific coast from southern Oregon to central California; some in the Southeast** · HABITAT **Foggy, rainy protected areas** · OTHER NAMES **California Redwood, Coast Redwood**

Stretching up, up, up into the fog, Redwoods are the tallest living things on Earth. They are also among the oldest living things, with some surviving for more than 2,000 years. These huge evergreens are called Redwoods for good reason: Their bark is thick and reddish brown. Their lower trunks are a single straight column for about 50 to 100 feet (15–30.5 m). Above that, they split into a branching spray of large limbs. It's as if several new trees are growing on top of one old tree. These long-lived plants resist disease and insects, and they can grow new sprouts from old stumps. Their worst enemies, at one time, were humans, who cut them down for their lovely wood. Now, most old-growth, or ancient, Redwoods are protected.

BE A TREE HUGGER!

Redwoods actually drink the fog that surrounds them. Fog turns into water droplets on their needles and drips to the forest floor. There, it waters the tree and the plants around it.

10s spotters

SMALL, BROWN, OVAL CONE HANGING FROM END OF TWIG

DARK GREEN NEEDLES IN FLAT SPRAYS

Giant Sequoia

Sequoiadendron giganteum
HEIGHT 150–290 ft (46–88.5 m) · **SHAPE** Tall and cone-shaped · **LEAVES** Scales · **CONES** Medium, brown, egg-shaped · **RANGE** California, western slopes of Sierra Nevada; some in the East as far north as Pennsylvania · **HABITAT** Sunny mountainsides in protected areas · **OTHER NAME** Sierra Redwood

Redwoods may be the world's tallest, but Giant Sequoias are true giants: tall, wide, and heavy! The biggest ones are more than 300 feet (91.5 m) tall and 25 feet (7.5 m) wide at the bottom—as wide as some houses! They can weigh more than two million pounds (907,000 kg). Like their relatives the Redwoods (see opposite page), Giant Sequoias are very long-lived trees: The oldest dates back 3,500 years. Younger trees have branches all the way down to the ground, but older ones have a bare trunk until close to the top. Their bark is rough, reddish brown, and naturally fire-resistant. There aren't many of these amazing trees left. They live mainly in a few protected groves in central California.

BROWN, OVAL CONE ON SHORT STALK

BLUISH GREEN, SCALY LEAVES

NAME GAME

The scientific names of these two species are right on target—or almost. *Giganteum* means "giant," which certainly describes the enormous sequoia. *Sempervirens* means both "evergreen" and "always living." Redwoods don't live forever, but 2,000 years is not too bad.

TREE-MENDOUS: CHAMPION TREES!

Individual tree name: Hyperion
Common name: Redwood
Scientific name: *Sequoia sempervirens*
Height: 379.1 feet (115.5 m)
Location: Redwood National and State Parks, California, U.S.A. This tree is about twice as tall as the Statue of Liberty.

SOME UNITED STATES FORESTS HAVE TREES TALLER THAN A 35-STORY BUILDING OR ALMOST AS OLD AS THE ANCIENT PYRAMIDS OF EGYPT.

Trees rule! They include the tallest, largest, and oldest plants on Earth. Many of these record-breakers live in North America, from the dry West to the swampy South. One tree is also among the most dangerous plants. If you see it, steer clear!

Oldest

Common name: Intermountain Bristlecone Pine
Scientific name: *Pinus longaeva*
Age: 5,065 years
Location: White Mountains of California, U.S.A.
This is the oldest single-trunk tree in the world.
Its exact location is kept secret to protect it.

Largest Tree From a Single Root

Individual tree name: Pando
Common name: Quaking Aspen
Scientific name: *Populus tremuloides*
Area: 106 acres (43 ha)
Total weight: Almost 13 million
pounds (5.9 million kg)
Location: Utah, U.S.A.
Pando has more than 40,000 trunks
growing from a single root.

Largest Single Tree

Individual tree name: General Sherman
Common name: Giant Sequoia
Scientific name: *Sequoiadendron giganteum*
Volume: 52,500 cubic feet (1,487 cubic m)
Distance around trunk at the ground: 102.6 feet
(31.3 m)
Location: Sequoia National Park, California, U.S.A.
General Sherman weighs as much as 64 medium-size
military tanks.

Most Dangerous

Common name: Manchineel
Scientific name: *Hippomane mancinella*
Location: Southern Florida to South America
Manchineel trees are very nasty. Their sap blisters your
skin. Their sweet fruit is poisonous. When they are
burned, their smoke can blind you. Stay away!

Taxodium distichum HEIGHT 65–130 ft (20–40 m) · SHAPE
Cone-shaped or irregular · LEAVES 0.75-in (2-cm) needles · CONES
Small, round, wrinkled · RANGE Southeast to Mississippi River
· HABITAT Swamps, creeks, other wet areas · OTHER NAMES
Swamp-cypress, Southern-cypress, Red-cypress,
Yellow-cypress

This tall conifer loves the water.
You'll find it growing in swampy
ground in warm, damp areas of the
Southeast. From a wide base, the
Baldcypress's trunk grows up into a
slender column. Its needlelike leaves
fan out like feathers from their branchlets.
In autumn, the needles and branchlets turn
red-brown and drop from the tree. Baldcypress
trees are useful to humans and animals. Their
wood is used for cabinets and roofs. Turkeys,
squirrels, and ducks eat their seeds, while frogs
and salamanders breed among their roots. Bald
eagles and ospreys nest in their crowns.

BE A TREE HUGGER!

These trees have knees!
In flooded areas around
Baldcypresses, little wooden
knobs rise out of the water.
These "knees" grow from the
wide-spreading Baldcypress
roots. Scientists think that
the portion above water
probably helps the tree get
oxygen, while the rest of
the knee joins the root
system underwater to anchor
the tree more firmly to
the ground.

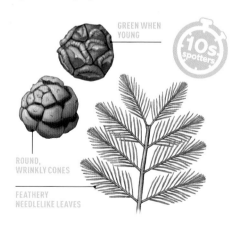

GREEN WHEN
YOUNG

10s
Spotters

ROUND,
WRINKLY CONES

FEATHERY
NEEDLELIKE LEAVES

EXPERT'S CIRCLE

DON'T BE FOOLED The Pond-cypress and the Baldcypress have similar trunks. Both trees like
wet areas. To tell the trees apart, check their leaves. Baldcypresses have needlelike leaves. Pond-cypress
leaves are scaly and stick up from the branchlets.

Arborvitae

Thuja occidentalis HEIGHT **40–65 ft (12–20 m)** • SHAPE **Cone-shaped** • LEAVES **Scales** • CONES **Oval, upright** • RANGE **Eastern Canada, south to Iowa and South Carolina** • HABITAT **Cool, wet areas in swamps or shorelines; cliffs** • OTHER NAMES **Eastern White Cedar, Northern White-Cedar, Swamp Cedar, Eastern Arborvitae**

The Arborvitae is a slow-growing tree that can live for more than a thousand years. This medium-size, densely leaved conifer likes cool, damp soil. In some places, it grows right out of cliffs. Arborvitae leaves are small, pointy scales that grow in fanlike sprays and give off a spicy-smelling oil when crushed. The Arborvitae is a particularly useful tree. Its oil is used in some perfumes and cleaners. The Ojibwa people have made the tree's inner bark and twigs into soups, as well as into teas that are said to relieve headaches.

TINY, SCALY LEAVES ON FANLIKE BRANCHLETS

OVAL, FLOWERLIKE CONES ON CURVED STALKS

DANGER!

Some people make medicines or drinks out of leaves or bark. Don't ever try this yourself. You could get very sick!

NAME GAME

"Arborvitae" means "tree of life" in Latin. It gained that name after Ojibwa healers taught 16th-century explorer Jacques Cartier how to use its leaves to treat scurvy, a deadly disease. It turns out that Arborvitae leaves contain vitamin C, the cure for scurvy.

Pacific Silver Fir

Abies amabilis HEIGHT 60–150 ft (18.5–46 m) · SHAPE **Slender and conical** · LEAVES **1.5-in (4-cm) needles** · CONES **Cylindrical, upright** · RANGE **Alaska to northwestern California** · HABITAT **Cool, moist valleys and hillsides in coastal forests** · OTHER NAMES **Silver Fir, Cascades Fir**

A tall, glossy green conifer, the Pacific Silver Fir is a handsome tree. Like all firs, it does not like hot, humid summers. This fir grows near the cool Pacific coast, where it is a home to owls, small rodents, and mountain goats. The tree's wood is soft and weak, so it is often sliced up to use in plywood. Its needles grow in thick sprays. If you look closely, each one has a groove down the middle. The cones grow only on the tree's upper branches. Green when young, the cones turn purple with age and shatter completely to release their seeds.

DENSE, GREEN NEEDLES ATTACHED IN SPIRALS ON THE TWIG

Laugh Out Loud!

What kind of tree makes the warmest coat?

A fir!

Balsam Fir

Abies balsamea HEIGHT 40–60 ft (12–18.5 m) · SHAPE **Slender and conical** · LEAVES **1.25-in (3-cm) needles** · CONES **Large, upright, cylindrical** · RANGE **Central to eastern Canada, Great Lakes, New England** · HABITAT **Moist swamps and mountainsides** · OTHER NAMES **Canada Balsam, Eastern Fir**

The Balsam Fir's pointy shape and pleasant, piney smell make it a popular choice for Christmas trees and wreaths. This medium-size conifer is widespread in northeastern North America. Its needles spray out along its twigs. Like other firs, it has upright, purplish cones on its upper branches. The bark releases a sticky liquid or resin, known as Canada balsam. It makes a good glue that hikers and campers may use for repairing equipment and even gluing together cuts.

UPRIGHT CONE WITH POINTY BRACTS BETWEEN SCALES

SHINY DARK GREEN NEEDLES CURVING UP

Fraser Fir

Abies fraseri HEIGHT **30–80 ft (9–24.5 m)** SHAPE **Slender and conical** LEAVES **1-in (2.5-cm) needles** CONES **Medium to large, upright** RANGE **Southeast, Virginia to Tennessee** HABITAT **High Appalachian forests** OTHER NAMES **She-Balsam, Southern Balsam Fir, Mountain Balsam Fir**

Like the Balsam Fir, the Fraser Fir is often grown in Christmas tree farms. Outside of these farms, it's found only in the southeastern Appalachian Mountains. Once it was more widespread, but an insect called the balsam woolly adelgid has killed off many of the trees since the 20th century. This conifer has thick, shiny, dark green needles that curve up from the twig. Pointy green or brown bracts—little leaves—stick out between the scales on its cones.

UPRIGHT CONE WITH POINTY BRACTS BETWEEN SCALES

SHINY DARK GREEN NEEDLES CURVING UP

EXPERT'S CIRCLE

DON'T BE FOOLED

Balsam Firs and Fraser Firs look alike. How to tell them apart:
Location. Balsam Firs live in the North, while Fraser Firs live in the Southeast, often in a high area away from the coast.
Cones. Papery, leaflike bracts stick out of Fraser Fir cones, while Balsam Fir bracts are mostly hidden.

Grand Fir

Abies grandis HEIGHT 100–260 ft (30.5–79 m) · SHAPE Slender, sometimes round-topped · LEAVES 2-in (5-cm) needles · CONES Tall, upright, barrel-shaped · RANGE Pacific Northwest · HABITAT Rain forests in valleys and mountain slopes · OTHER NAMES Lowland White Fir, California Great Fir, Yellow Fir

This conifer is truly grand. It can grow more than 200 feet (61 m) tall in the Northwest's rain forests. Like many other firs, it has needles with a pleasant, piney smell. These needles grow in flat rows; the cones are smooth, upright, and barrel-shaped. The tree has been put to many uses through the years. Its wood is used in buildings. Native Americans used to burn the leaves to make a healing smoke. Some people even rubbed the tree's sap on their scalps to try to cure baldness!

BE A TREE HUGGER!

On the south slope of Oregon's Mount Hood, you can see the famous "Barlow Road snub trees." These Grand Fir tree stumps still show the marks where wagon train drivers on the Oregon Trail tied ropes around them. The slope was so steep that the drivers attached the wagons to the trees with ropes or chains and then lowered them slowly down the hill.

TALL, SMOOTH, BARREL-SHAPED CONES

SHINY DARK GREEN NEEDLES IN FLAT SPRAYS

10s spotters

California Red Fir

Abies magnifica HEIGHT 60–130 ft (18.5–40 m)
- SHAPE Tall, cone-shaped with short branches
- LEAVES 1.25-in (3-cm) needles - CONES Large,
barrel-shaped, rounded - RANGE Oregon to
California - HABITAT High up on mountainsides
- OTHER NAMES Red Fir, Shasta Red Fir

California Red Firs are big,
stately, long-lived coni-
fers. They're called "red"
because the older trees
have a reddish bark, but
their leaves are actually blue-
green. These sharp needles curve
up from their twigs like a brush. The
upright cones are purple or brown,
and in some varieties bracts (little
pointy leaves) stick out between the
cones' scales. Floating down from the
trees in the fall, the seeds are food
for mice and other little mammals.

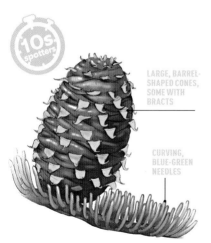

LARGE, BARREL-
SHAPED CONES,
SOME WITH
BRACTS

CURVING,
BLUE-GREEN
NEEDLES

TRY THIS!

MAKE A BARK RUBBING

Trees have all kinds of bark—
smooth, rough, ridged, or peeling. You can take home a picture
of a tree's bark by making a rub-
bing. You only need two items:
- 1 large crayon
- 2 or 3 sheets of thin drawing
paper

1. Peel all the paper off your
crayon.
2. Put the drawing paper up
against the bark of your
chosen tree.
3. Rub the side of the crayon up
and down and side to side
until the bark's pattern shows
through clearly. You may need
two or three tries.
4. Label your picture with the
common and scientific name
of the tree!

Tamarack

Larix laricina HEIGHT 40–80 ft (12–24.5 m) SHAPE Small to medium size, open and conical LEAVES 1-in (2.5-cm) needles in soft tufts CONES Small, brown, upright, egg-shaped RANGE Canada to northeastern United States and Great Lakes HABITAT Swampy forests OTHER NAMES Eastern Larch, American larch, Hackmatack

The Tamarack likes cool weather, so you'll find it only in northern areas. Its soft, green needles grow in tufts or clusters from a central point on the twig. This tree is one of the few deciduous conifers. Its leaves turn yellow in autumn and fall off, growing afresh in spring. Porcupines enjoy eating the inner bark. If they eat all the way around the tree, they can kill it.

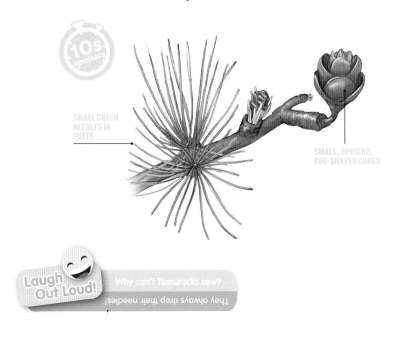

10s Spotters

SMALL GREEN NEEDLES IN TUFTS

SMALL, UPRIGHT, EGG-SHAPED CONES

Laugh Out Loud!

Why can't Tamaracks sew?

They always drop their needles!

White Spruce

Picea glauca HEIGHT **40–130 ft (12–40 m)** SHAPE
Medium to large, dense, cone-shaped LEAVES **0.5-in
(1.25-cm)** sharp, blue-green needles CONES **Small,
green, purplish, or brown; some drooping, others
upright** RANGE **Alaska, Canada, Great Lakes,
New England** HABITAT **Bogs, riverbanks,
northern forests, rocky hills** OTHER NAMES
Canada Spruce, Skunk Spruce, Cat Spruce

The White Spruce grows
farther north than any
other American tree.
These tough trees are
found from north of the
Arctic Circle down to Wisconsin,
Michigan, and Vermont. In some
places they are tall and impressive.
In others, such as near the tree line on moun-
tains, they are as small as shrubs. When crushed, the White Spruce's
blue-green needles give off a stinky odor, earning the tree some other
common names, such as Skunk Spruce or Cat Spruce.

MEDIUM, SLENDER,
FLEXIBLE CONES,
RANGING FROM
GREEN TO PURPLE
TO BROWN

SHORT BLUE-
GREEN NEEDLES
ALONG TWIGS

CONES HANG
DOWN; OPEN TO
DISPERSE SEEDS

BE A TREE HUGGER!

The White Spruce is the state
tree of South Dakota and the
provincial tree of Manitoba.

→ **LOOK FOR THIS** When no cones are present, you can tell a spruce apart from a fir by looking at the twigs.
When needles drop from a fir twig, the twig is smooth. When needles drop from a spruce twig, the twig is rough.

Black Spruce

Picea mariana **HEIGHT** 20–100 ft (6–30.5 m) · **SHAPE** Usually small to medium size, skinny, with drooping branches · **LEAVES** 0.5-in (1.25-cm) blue-green needles · **CONES** Small, oval, stiff, purplish to brown · **RANGE** Alaska through Canada to Great Lakes and New England · **HABITAT** Swamps, bogs, forests, mountains · **OTHER NAMES** Bog Spruce, Swamp Spruce

Like its relative the White Spruce (see page 31), this coni-fer can be found all over the far north. It grows slowly and sometimes looks thin and scrag-gly. In the coldest spots it may be only a few feet tall and an inch or two around. Unlike the White Spruce, the Black Spruce has blunt needles that release a piney, pleasant smell when crushed.

→LOOK FOR THIS

The **BLACK SPRUCE** doesn't always need seeds to repro-duce. Where its lower limbs touch the ground, they some-times take root. New, smaller trees grow up from the roots in a circle around the parent tree.

SHORT BLUE-GREEN NEEDLES COVERING THE TWIG

SMALL, STIFF, OVAL, BROWN CONES, OFTEN CLUSTERED TOGETHER

Blue Spruce

Picea pungens HEIGHT 65–100 ft (20–30.5 m) · SHAPE cone-shaped · LEAVES 0.5-in (1.25-cm) blue-green or silvery blue needles · CONES Long, slender ovals; glossy brown · RANGE Rocky Mountains from Idaho to Arizona and New Mexico · HABITAT High up on slopes and along streams · OTHER NAMES Colorado Spruce, Silver Spruce

The Blue Spruce's neat shape and silvery blue color make it a popular tree for yards and Christmas trees. In the wild, it's a green, slow-growing mountain plant. Some Blue Spruces live to be up to 600 years old. Trees that are grown for holiday trees or for yards are more likely to have blue or silver leaves, but watch out: Those needles are sharp!

Engelmann Spruce

Picea engelmannii HEIGHT 80–165 ft (24.5–50.5 m) · SHAPE Tall, dense, narrow, cone-shaped · LEAVES 1-in (2.5-cm) blue-green needles · CONES Medium size, orange-brown to purple-brown · RANGE Western Canada to New Mexico · HABITAT Higher up on mountain slopes · OTHER NAMES Engelmann Blue Spruce, Rocky Mountain White Spruce

These big conifers are common in Rocky Mountain forests. Their small, dark needles grow thickly on long twigs and give off a sharp smell like medicine when crushed. Engelmann spruces are useful from the inside out. Instrument makers shape their soft wood into guitars and parts for pianos. Sometimes their young cones are eaten raw or added to breads. Even the seeds can be eaten.

Red Spruce

Picea rubens HEIGHT 60–80 ft (18.5–24.5 m)
SHAPE Broad, cone-shaped LEAVES 0.75-in (2-cm)
needles CONES Small, red-brown, egg-shaped
RANGE Eastern Canada to North Carolina HABITAT
Mountain forests OTHER NAMES He-Balsam, Eastern
Spruce, Yellow Spruce

A medium-size conifer, the Red Spruce is a common tree of northeastern forests. Curving yellowish needles cover its twigs. Its light, straight-grained wood is often used in buildings, as well as in guitars and pianos. Into the 20th century, people made chewing gum out of its sticky resin. The Red Spruce is sensitive to air pollution, so in some higher mountains the trees are dying off.

BE A TREE HUGGER!

You might not like a diet of tree needles, but the spruce grouse loves it. This plump bird mainly eats the needles of spruce trees and other conifers. In summer, it hunts for needles on the ground. In winter, it plucks them from the trees.

CURVED, BRIGHT GREEN, SHARP NEEDLES

SMALL, EGG-SHAPED, RED-BROWN CONES

Sitka Spruce

Picea sitchensis HEIGHT **150–200 ft (46–61 m)** SHAPE **Tall, broad cone-shaped crown** LEAVES **1-in (2.5-cm) needles** CONES **Long, slender, orange-brown** RANGE **Pacific coast from southern Alaska to Northern California** HABITAT **Wet coastal forests** OTHER NAMES **Coast Spruce, Tideland Spruce**

Sitka Spruces are grand trees. These conifers are among the largest trees on the planet, with one record-holder growing more than 300 feet (91.5 m) tall. They prefer cool, damp, but open areas. Sitka Spruces have sharp, dark-green needles on sweeping branches, and their trunks are wide at the base—the better to hold them up! Their wood is so light and strong that it was used in airplanes in World Wars I and II.

CONES; GREEN WHEN YOUNG

FLAT, DARK-GREEN, SHARP NEEDLES

SLENDER, ORANGE-BROWN CONES

→LOOK FOR THIS

You might see several **SITKA SPRUCES** in a row growing from roots that curve up over a hollow space. This happens when seeds drop onto a log called a "nurse log." New trees grow up from the seeds while the log rots away. After a while, the log is gone, but the trees are still there.

STIFF, OLIVE TO GRAY-GREEN
NEEDLES IN PAIRS

Jack Pine

Pinus banksiana HEIGHT **55–65 ft (17–20 m)** · SHAPE **Small to medium, thin cone-shaped crown** · LEAVES **2-in (5-cm) needles in pairs** · CONES **Small, slender, curved** · RANGE **Canada, Great Lakes, New England to Illinois** · HABITAT **Sandy soil, rocky ground, soil over permafrost** · OTHER NAME **Scrub Pine**

A scraggly northern conifer, the Jack Pine has a remarkable life cycle: It needs fire to reproduce. Its seeds are trapped inside sticky cones. When the heat around the cones reaches 120°F (49°C) or more, the cones pop open and release the winged seeds. Tree experts called foresters who take care of Jack Pines deliberately set fires to start new trees growing.

Lodgepole Pine

Pinus contorta HEIGHT **30–100 ft (9–30.5 m)** · SHAPE **Inland: tall and slender; coastal: shrubby and twisted** · LEAVES **1–3-in (2.5–7.5-cm) needles in pairs** · CONES **Small, oval, prickly** · RANGE **Alaska to Southern California; Rocky Mountains** · HABITAT **Forests with moist soil** · OTHER NAMES **Tamarack Pine, Scrub Pine**

These widespread western conifers will grow in many habitats. You can find them in warm or cold climates and rocky, sandy, or ashy soils. They come in different shapes and sizes. On inland mountains, they are tall and straight. Near the coast, they are short and crooked. In either case, look for their paired, short needles and prickly cones. The inland variety releases its seeds during fires, like its close relative the Jack Pine (see above).

CURVED, YELLOW-GREEN NEEDLES IN PAIRS

OVAL CONES; GREEN WHEN YOUNG, BROWN AND PRICKLY WHEN MATURE

NAME GAME

This pine is called "lodgepole" because Native Americans use its thin, flexible branches to build tepees.

Shortleaf Pine

Pinus echinata HEIGHT **70–100 ft (21.5–30.5 m)**
- SHAPE **Medium to tall, cone-shaped or rounded**
- LEAVES **3–4.5-in (7.5–11.5-cm) needles in twos and threes** CONES **Small, oval, prickly**
- RANGE **Mid-Atlantic, Southeast to Texas**
- HABITAT **Floodplains to mountain slopes**
- OTHER NAMES **Yellow Pine, Shortstraw Pine**

The Shortleaf Pine is a wide-ranging tree, growing from Pennsylvania to Texas. It's an important tree for builders, who use its wood for floors, roof beams, and pulp. It's also important to the endangered red-cockaded woodpecker, which nests in old-growth Shortleaf Pines. Although it's called "shortleaf," this pine's needles are short only when compared to those of other southern pines. The leaves are actually medium-long and grow in pairs or triplets on the twig.

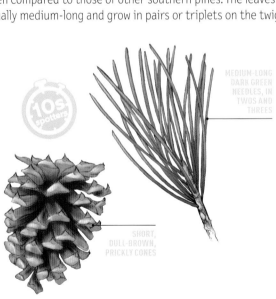

MEDIUM-LONG DARK GREEN NEEDLES, IN TWOS AND THREES

SHORT, DULL-BROWN, PRICKLY CONES

Piñon Pine

Pinus edulis HEIGHT 15–40 ft (4.5–12 m) · SHAPE Short, shrubby, gnarled, dense · LEAVES 0.75–2-in (2–5-cm) needles, mostly in pairs · CONES Small, rounded, with thick scales · RANGE Southwest · HABITAT Dry mountains and plateaus · OTHER NAMES Pinyon, Two-needle Pine, Colorado Pinyon

A slow-growing, shrubby conifer, the Piñon Pine does well in dry places—even on the rim of the Grand Canyon. It is a favorite food source for humans and birds alike. Its bumpy cones hold big, tasty seeds known as pine nuts (though they aren't actually nuts). When the cones get older, they open up. Pinyon jays and other birds pluck out the seeds and stash them in hiding places to eat later. The seeds that they forget grow into new trees. People also collect the seeds to eat in salads and sauces.

BE A TREE HUGGER!

You need patience if you want to harvest pine nuts. Piñons start making seeds only when they get to be 75 to 100 years old. A good seed crop comes every four to seven years.

SMALL, SHINY, BUMPY CONES

SHORT TO MEDIUM DARK GREEN NEEDLES, IN PAIRS, SOMETIMES IN ONES OR THREES

Slash Pine

Pinus elliottii HEIGHT 60–100 ft (18.5–30.5 m) · SHAPE
Medium to tall with high, rounded crown · LEAVES 8–12-in
(20.5–30.5-cm) needles in twos or threes · CONES Long,
oval, prickly · RANGE Florida and coastal Southeast
· HABITAT Moist coastal plains, edges of ponds
· OTHER NAMES Yellow Slash Pine, Swamp Pine

Fast-growing Slash Pines
have straight, branchless
trunks up to a high crown
with long needles. They're
called "slash" because they
frequently live in stretches of
overgrown swampland, known
as slashes. Slash Pine bark peels
off in large flakes. Because they have
heavy, strong wood, Slash Pines are often
cut down for lumber.

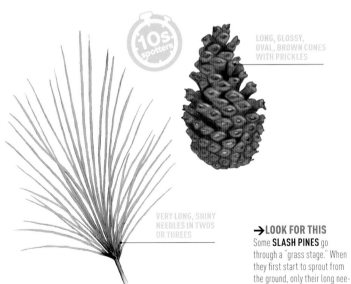

LONG, GLOSSY,
OVAL, BROWN CONES
WITH PRICKLES

VERY LONG, SHINY
NEEDLES IN TWOS
OR THREES

→ **LOOK FOR THIS**
Some **SLASH PINES** go
through a "grass stage." When
they first start to sprout from
the ground, only their long needles are visible. The clump of
needles looks like a tuft of
grass, not a tree.

TREE-MENDOUS: AMAZING SEEDS!

Acorn

All oak trees grow acorns. Under their neat little caps, inside their shiny shells, acorns hold one or two oak seeds. Animals such as jays and squirrels love to eat acorns. After the nuts drop from the trees, animals pick them up and carry them to a secret place where they stash them to eat later. If they forget to eat them, new trees can grow from this spot.

SEEDS ARE NATURALLY SPREAD BY WIND OR ANIMALS AND GROW INTO FORESTS LIKE THESE.

Trees can't pick up their roots and walk around to spread their seeds. They rely on animals, wind, water—and pure gravity—to do the job for them. Tree seeds come in an astonishing range of sizes and shapes, all to help them make the move to a new home.

Maple Wings

Curved, leafy wings enclose each maple seed. Botanists call them "keys" or "samaras." When the maple tree releases its seeds, the samaras twirl and fly on the wind. They can carry the seeds far away to start a new tree.

Cherry

Cherry and other fruit trees hide their seeds inside a sweet, fleshy covering. The bright colors and tasty flavors attract birds and other animals, which eat the fruit. The animals then go about their business and leave behind the seeds in their droppings.

Coconut

Coconuts, covered by a rough husk, are among the biggest seeds in the world. Be careful if you stand under a coconut palm—a falling seed might give you a good whack on the head! Coconuts are hollow and can float, sometimes traveling from one island to another on the waves.

Sugar Pine

Pinus lambertiana HEIGHT 100–200 ft (30.5–61 m) · SHAPE Very tall, slender, with large branches · LEAVES 2.5–4-in (6.5–10-cm) needles in groups of five · CONES Very long, oval, brown · RANGE Oregon to California · HABITAT Mountain forests · OTHER NAMES None

This towering conifer is the largest pine tree. In sheer tree size, it comes close to the Giant Sequoia. One Sugar Pine in Yosemite National Park is 273 feet (83 m) tall. Even its cones are huge, averaging 16 inches (40.5 cm) long as they dangle from the ends of the heavy branches. The Sugar Pine's light, strong wood is widely used to make doors and window frames.

10s spotters

MEDIUM BLUE-GREEN NEEDLES IN BUNDLES OF FIVE

VERY LONG BROWN CONES DANGLING FROM BRANCHES

NAME GAME

Sugar Pines get their sweet name from their sugary resin, a kind of sap that oozes out in sticky drops when the tree is cut.

Singleleaf Piñon

Pinus monophylla HEIGHT 16–40 ft (5–12 m) · SHAPE Small to medium, rounded or irregular · LEAVES 0.75–2-in (2–5-cm) single needles · CONES Small, rounded oval, with thick scales · RANGE Idaho to California and the Southwest · HABITAT Dry mountain woodlands and plateaus · OTHER NAMES None

Small and slow growing, Singleleaf Piñons are trees of the dry western states. They are called "singleleaf" because their needles don't grow in bundles, unlike on other pine trees. Like its relative the Piñon Pine (see page 38), the Singleleaf Piñon produces tasty seeds, known as pine nuts, in its cones. Birds such as the Clark's nutcracker and mammals such as the white-footed pinyon mouse like the seeds, too.

SHORT, SINGLE BLUE-GREEN NEEDLES

SMALL, GREEN TO BROWN, THICK-SCALED CONES

→LOOK FOR THIS

DWARF MISTLETOE is not a holiday decoration. It's a parasite—it lives by sucking water and minerals out of pine trees in the Southwest. Dwarf mistletoe will hurt or kill the tree it feeds on. Look for knobby growths, ranging from green to orange, in the tree's crown.

Western White Pine

MEDIUM TO LONG BLUE-GREEN NEEDLES IN BUNDLES OF FIVE

LONG, NARROW, BROWN CONES WITH THIN, CURVED SCALES

Pinus monticola HEIGHT 100–200 ft (30.5–61 m) · SHAPE Very tall, narrow, with large branches · LEAVES 2–4-in (5–10-cm) needles in clusters of five · CONES Long, reddish brown, slender · RANGE Western Canada to the U.S. Northwest and California · HABITAT Mountain forests, wetlands, coasts · OTHER NAMES Mountain White Pine, Idaho Pine, Silver Pine

The Western White Pine is a tall, fast-growing tree with a straight, massive trunk. After a forest fire clears out other trees, these pine trees are among the first to take hold and spread. Their light, straight-grained wood is prized for cabinets, moldings, and trim in houses. An invasive fungus called white pine blister rust, which only occurs when currants or gooseberries grow nearby, has killed many trees in some areas. Bears sometimes damage the trees by tearing into them to eat their sweet sapwood.

VERY LONG, SLENDER, FLEXIBLE
NEEDLES, MOSTLY IN THREES

Longleaf Pine

Pinus palustris HEIGHT **80–120 ft (24.5–36.5 m)** · SHAPE **Tall, slender, with short irregular crown** · LEAVES **8–12-in (20.5–30.5-cm) or longer needles in twos or threes** · CONES **Large, oval, brown, and prickly** · RANGE **Southeast from Virginia to Texas** · HABITAT **Warm, wet coastal plains** · OTHER NAMES **Southern Yellow Pine, Longstraw Pine, Georgia Pine**

EXPERT'S CIRCLE

DON'T BE FOOLED

Longleaf and Slash Pines (see page 39) look alike. To tell them apart, look at the ends of their branches. Longleaf Pine branches have a thick, curving tip; Slash Pine branches are slender out to their ends.

This tall, skinny pine is called "longleaf" for a reason: It has the longest needles of any eastern pine, 8–12 inches (20.5–30.5 cm) or longer in length. The tree starts life as a grasslike tuft of needles growing from the ground. This seedling sets up a root system before it starts to grow upward. Endangered red-cockaded woodpeckers live in Longleaf Pines and razorback hogs eat the seedlings. These trees have been vanishing as their coastal habitat was cut down to plant crops, and the trees were used for their wood and resin. Foresters are now working on restoring them.

Ponderosa Pine

Pinus ponderosa HEIGHT **60–140 ft (18.5–42.5 m)** · SHAPE **Very tall, straight, with clear trunk and cone-shaped crown** · LEAVES **5–11-in (12.5–28-cm) needles, three to a bundle** · CONES **Medium size, reddish brown, egg-shaped, prickly** · RANGE **Across the West, from the Pacific to the Rockies** · HABITAT **Forests from sea level to mountain slopes** · OTHER NAMES **Western Yellow Pine, Yellow Pine, Blackjack**

MEDIUM TO LONG,
SHARP, YELLOW-GREEN
NEEDLES IN THREES

The Ponderosa Pine is a tall, majestic tree found throughout the western United States. It can grow in a wide range of places, thriving in hot or cold weather, on wet mountains, or in dry desertlike lands. Older trees have a bright orangish bark whose sharp plates are outlined in black. Builders use the wood for cabinets and other construction.

Red Pine

Pinus resinosa HEIGHT 50–80 ft (15–24.5 m)
· SHAPE **Medium to tall, with a dense rounded crown**
· LEAVES **4–6.5-in (10–16.5-cm) needles, in pairs**
· CONES **Small, brown, egg-shaped, not prickly**
· RANGE **Eastern Canada and northeastern United States to the Great Lakes and Virginia** · HABITAT **Cold forests with sandy soil** · OTHER NAMES **Norway Pine, Eastern Red Pine**

Named for its reddish bark, the Red Pine likes chilly weather, sunny spots, and sandy, acid soils. In the wild, it grows best when fire clears out other trees, leaving space for Red Pine seedlings. These good-looking trees are also popular plantings in parks and yards. Unlike the leaves of many pines, its needles are so stiff that they snap when bent.

SMALL,
EGG-SHAPED,
BROWN
CONES WITH
SMOOTH
EDGES

LIGHT RED FLOWER
CLUSTER AT
BRANCH TIP

MEDIUM-SIZE,
BRITTLE
NEEDLES
IN PAIRS

NAME GAME

The Red Pine is often called the Norway Pine—but why? Although the tree is native to America, it may have reminded early European settlers of the Norway Spruce back home.

Eastern White Pine

Pinus strobus HEIGHT 50–150 ft (15–46 m) · SHAPE Very tall, with long, widely spaced branches · LEAVES 2.5–5-in (6.5–12.5-cm) needles in bundles of five · CONES Very long, slender, brown, with smooth edges · RANGE Eastern Canada through eastern United States and Great Lakes, south to Georgia · HABITAT Cool upland forests · OTHER NAMES Weymouth Pine, Northern White Pine

The Eastern White Pine is the tallest pine in the East. Its massive form impressed early European settlers, who took seeds back to England in the 17th century. Its strong, straight wood impressed builders, too, who used it for furniture and ships' masts. Now, very few old trees remain standing. However, younger trees are widespread in forests throughout eastern North America.

BE A TREE HUGGER!

To the Iroquois people, the Eastern White Pine is known as the "tree of peace." Its bundle of five needles symbolizes the five nations of the Iroquois, working together as one.

VERY LONG, NARROW, BROWN CONES, SOMETIMES CURVED

MEDIUM-SIZE, SOFT, BLUE-GREEN NEEDLES IN CLUSTERS OF FIVE

Loblolly Pine

Pinus taeda HEIGHT 60–140 ft (18.5–42.5 m) · SHAPE Tall, with a large cone-shaped crown · LEAVES 6–9-in (15–23-cm) needles in threes · CONES Short to medium-long, light brown, with prickles · RANGE Southern and eastern coast from New Jersey to Texas · HABITAT Fields, forests, swamps · OTHER NAME Oldfield Pine

MEDIUM TO LONG YELLOW-GREEN NEEDLES IN THREES

Tall and fast growing, the Loblolly Pine is found all over the coastal South. The name "Loblolly" comes from a southern word meaning "swamp" or "bog," and it's true that the tree likes to grow in swampy areas. Its other name, Oldfield Pine, refers to the fact that these trees are often the first to grow back in abandoned fields. The Loblolly is often planted in tree farms and cut for its useful wood.

BE A TREE HUGGER!

Loblolly seeds traveled all the way to the moon with Apollo 14 astronaut Stuart Roosa in 1971. When they returned, the seeds had grown into seedlings. These "moon trees" were planted all over the United States—including at the White House!

Virginia Pine

Pinus virginiana HEIGHT 25–50 ft (7.5–15 m) · SHAPE Small to medium size, with rounded or flat scraggly crown · LEAVES 1–3-in (2.5–7.5-cm) needles in pairs · CONES Small, egg-shaped, prickly · RANGE New York to Ohio and south to Mississippi · HABITAT Fields, slopes, mountain foothills and ridges · OTHER NAMES Scrub Pine, Jersey Pine

SHORT, TWISTED, GRAY-GREEN NEEDLES IN PAIRS

SMALL, EGG-SHAPED, WOODY, PRICKLY CONES

The Virginia Pine is one tough little tree. It lives where other trees can't, such as on dry, barren, sandy soil. In these poor conditions, it may be especially small and scrubby looking. Like the Loblolly Pine, the Virginia Pine is one of the first trees to grow back in abandoned fields. Woodpeckers often live in older trees, pecking out nests in their trunks.

Douglas-fir

Pseudotsuga menziesii HEIGHT 80–200 ft (24.5–61 m) · SHAPE Medium to very tall, cone-shaped · LEAVES 1-in (2.5-cm) needles in rows · CONES Medium size, light-brown, oval, with bracts sticking out · RANGE West Coast to Rocky Mountains · HABITAT Moist, shady forests · OTHER NAMES Douglas-spruce, Oregon-pine

At their tallest, Douglas-firs are among the biggest trees in the United States. These massive conifers are native to the West, but they are planted in cool places across the country. They are particularly valuable for their lumber. Douglas-fir wood is used for house beams, poles, and to make paper.

SHORT, FLATTENED NEEDLES IN ROWS

MEDIUM-SIZE, OVAL, LIGHT-BROWN CONES WITH THREE-POINTED BRACTS STICKING OUT FROM SCALES

EXPERT'S CIRCLE

DON'T BE FOOLED Despite its name, the Douglas-fir is not a true fir tree. It belongs to its own genus with just five species. You can tell the difference between Douglas-firs and true firs by looking at their cones. Douglas-fir cones hang down from their branches. True fir cones stand up straight from upper branches of their trees.

Eastern Hemlock

Tsuga canadensis HEIGHT 60–100 ft (18.5–30.5 m) · SHAPE Medium to tall, cone-shaped crown with slightly drooping branches · LEAVES 0.5-in (1.25-cm) needles in flat rows · CONES Small, brown, oval · RANGE Eastern Canada, Minnesota through northeastern states, to mountains of Georgia and Alabama · HABITAT Shady forests from sea level to low slopes · OTHER NAME Canada Hemlock

The graceful Eastern Hemlock is often found in shady forests along ridges and mountain slopes. Early settlers valued it for a substance called tannin in its bark, which was used to make leather out of animal skin. Today, the trees are threatened by a pest called the hemlock woolly adelgid. This tiny insect, native to Asia and introduced into the United States in the 20th century, feeds on the tree's twigs and eventually kills it.

SHORT, FLAT, DARK GREEN NEEDLES

Pacific Yew

Taxus brevifolia HEIGHT 15–50 ft (4.5–15 m)
- SHAPE Small, with long drooping branches
- LEAVES 0.75-in (2-cm) flat needles in rows
- CONES Tiny, green, growing into red, berrylike
arils · RANGE Alaska to central California, and
western Canada to Idaho · HABITAT Moist forests, mountains · OTHER NAME Western Yew

This small, slow-growing conifer looks either like a small tree or a shrub with many trunks. It has long branches that can droop toward the ground. Its seeds grow out of the small, young cones and are covered by a red berrylike structure called an aril. Arils are fruity seed coverings that attract animals to eat the seeds, which are then distributed through the animals' droppings. The Pacific Yew has attractive, fine-grained wood that can be made into musical instruments and archery bows.

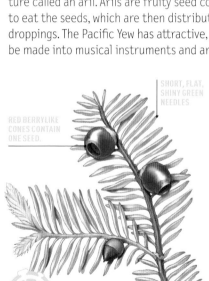

SHORT, FLAT, SHINY GREEN NEEDLES

RED BERRYLIKE CONES CONTAIN ONE SEED.

BE A TREE HUGGER!

Pacific Yews are both killers and healers. Their seeds, bark, and leaves are poisonous. Even their pollen causes bad allergies. But scientists also use their bark to make a powerful anticancer drug called paclitaxel.

DANGER!

Never eat any part of a Pacific Yew. The seeds may be tasty to animals, but to people they are poisonous. So are the bark and leaves.

TREE-MENDOUS: THE ONE AND ONLY GINKGO!

THE *GINKGO BILOBA*, OR GINKGO, IS IDENTIFIED BY ITS WIDE, FAN-SHAPED YELLOW LEAVES AND PLUMLIKE, SMELLY FRUIT.

The Ginkgo, with its fan-shaped leaves, is a dinosaur among trees. In fact, it is older than the dinosaurs: This genus has survived almost unchanged for at least 270 million years. The Ginkgo is considered a conifer, but it is the only tree in its own division of plants, Ginkgophyta. The male seeds grow inside a cone, and the female seeds are inside a fruit that looks like a small plum. Though Ginkgoes are native to China, they can now be found around the world. As beautiful as they are, they have one big drawback. When the fruits of the female trees drop to the ground and decay, they stink like rotting food. That's why the ancient Ginkgo is also sometimes called the "stinkbomb tree." The Gingko has other stinky, prehistoric cousins. Check them out here.

Wollemia Pine

Scientific name: *Wollemia nobilis*
Age of genus: 200 million years
Range: Eastern Australia
Height: 82–131 feet (25–40 m)
Leaves: Medium-size flat spears in feathery rows
Cones: Small, slender, brown

Dawn Redwood

Scientific name: *Metasequoia glyptostroboides*
Age of genus: 50 million years
Range: Central and western China, now grown in North America
Height: 70–100 feet (21.5–30.5 m)
Leaves: Small needles in opposite rows
Cones: Small, round, brown

Monkey Puzzle

Scientific name: *Araucaria araucana*
Age of genus: 200 million years
Range: Chile, Argentina, now grown in North America
Height: 50–80 feet (15–24.5 m)
Leaves: Thicky, scaly, sharp-edged
Cones: Medium size, slender, barrel-shaped

Bigleaf Maple

Acer macrophyllum HEIGHT 30–80 ft (9–24.5 m)
- SHAPE Medium size; straight, stout trunk; rounded crown
- LEAVES Opposite, simple; 6–12 in (15–30.5 cm), shiny dark green, with 5 deep lobes • FLOWERS Yellow-green, sweet-smelling, in hanging clusters • FRUITS Samaras in pairs, in long clusters • RANGE West Coast from Canada to Southern California • HABITAT Moist forests, stream banks
- OTHER NAMES Oregon Maple, Broadleaf Maple

This tree's name is no joke: It has really big leaves. With five deep lobes, the leaves are the size of a dinner plate: They grow up to a foot (30.5 cm) wide and a foot long and hang from a long stem. The Bigleaf Maple lives in damp, mountainous forests and around streams and rivers. Sometimes mosses and ferns grow right on its trunk. Its light-brown wood is often used to make musical instruments, furniture, and cabinets.

YELLOW-GREEN, FRAGRANT, HANGING FLOWERS

VERY LARGE, DARK GREEN, FIVE-LOBED LEAVES

SAMARAS IN PAIRS

NAME GAME

You might know the flying, spinning maple fruit as a wing, key, helicopter, whirlybird, or spinning jenny. But its official name is samara, which comes from the Latin word for "elm seed."

Box Elder

Acer negundo HEIGHT 30–70 ft (9–21.5 m) · SHAPE
Small to medium size, short trunk, rounded crown · LEAVES
Opposite, compound; 6 in (15 cm), 3 to 9 leaflets on a
twig · FLOWERS Small clusters on a twig, pink or yellow
· FRUITS Samaras in pairs, often in long clusters
· RANGE Great Plains to eastern United States;
scattered regions in the West · HABITAT River
bottoms, stream banks · OTHER NAMES Manitoba
Maple, Ash-leaf Maple

It's called a Box Elder, but
this small broadleaf is really a
maple tree. It earned its common name because its soft wood is
good only for making boxes, and its
leaves look like those of Elder shrubs. The
Box Elder is the only native maple with com-
pound leaves, which can grow in groups of three, five, or more leaflets.
Often the leaves and seeds remain on the trees through the winter, and
the seeds provide food for birds. People often plant this fast-growing
tree in cities. However, it's not ideal there because its branches are
weak and can drop in a storm.

OPPOSITE,
COMPOUND,
SMOOTH, WITH
TOOTHED EDGES

10s
spotters

SAMARAS IN
PAIRS, OFTEN IN
LONG CLUSTERS

EXPERT'S CIRCLE

DON'T BE FOOLED Three-leafed Box Elder seedlings look
a lot like poison ivy—even though Box Elder is not poisonous. However,
poison ivy has alternate leaves, not opposite leaves. When in doubt,
don't touch! Remember: Leaves of three, let it be.

Red Maple

Acer rubrum HEIGHT 60–80 ft (18.5–24.5 m) · SHAPE Medium size, straight, with dense curved crown · LEAVES Opposite, simple, 2.5–5 in (6.5–12.5 cm), with 3 or 5 lobes, toothed edges · FLOWERS Red or yellow on bare branches · FRUITS Small samaras in pairs · RANGE Eastern United States · HABITAT Sea level to mountains, moist soil · OTHER NAMES Swamp Maple, Scarlet Maple

The Red Maple is a favorite tree of many people in the eastern United States. It is found all over, from yards to woods, and from valleys to mountains. And it is red, red, red. Its young leaves are red, its twigs are red, it fruits are red, and its flowers are red. Only its bark is grayish. In spring, it is one of the earliest trees to flower. In autumn, its leaves turn yellow to a brilliant scarlet.

MEDIUM LEAVES, WITH THREE OR FIVE SHALLOW LOBES; DARK GREEN ABOVE AND PALE BELOW IN SUMMER, SCARLET IN AUTUMN

YELLOW OR RED FLOWERS

....

Japanese Maple

TREE HAS DOME-LIKE SHAPE

Acer palmatum HEIGHT 15–20 ft (4.5–6 m) · SHAPE Small, with short trunk and wide, curving crown · LEAVES Opposite, simple, 2–4 in (5–10 cm), with 5 to 11 pointed lobes · FLOWERS Red in clusters · FRUITS Samaras in pairs · RANGE Native to Japan; across the United States · HABITAT Moist soils in sun or part shade · OTHER NAMES None

Just as their name suggests, Japanese Maples originally came from Japan. Now, though, you can find them across much of the United States. Because of their graceful, spreading shape and colorful leaves, they have been bred in hundreds of varieties to be planted in parks and yards. Some are as small as shrubs. Many varieties have purple leaves year-round. In the autumn, they often turn a brilliant red, yellow, or bronze color.

WIDE LEAVES WITH POINTED LOBES ARE GREEN, LIGHT RED, OR DEEP RED.

BE A TREE HUGGER!

Japanese maples are often used as bonsai—trees that are carefully cut and shaped to grow in containers. A bonsai tree may be only one or two feet (30.5–61 cm) high.

Silver Maple

Acer saccharinum HEIGHT 50–80 ft
(15–24.5 m) · SHAPE Medium to tall, with a short
trunk and wide crown · LEAVES Opposite, simple,
5–7 in (12.5–18 cm), with 5 lobes · FLOWERS Red
to green clusters · FRUITS Large samaras in
pairs · RANGE Eastern to midwestern United
States · HABITAT Wet areas such as rivers,
swamps, and drainage ditches · OTHER
NAMES None

The Silver Maple is a tree in a hurry. It grows up to seven feet (2 m) a year, and this makes it a popular choice for yards and streets. Its leaves are green on top but pale silver underneath. When the wind blows, they flip up to show their silvery undersides, giving the tree its common name. However, many people regret planting the Silver Maple. Its branches are brittle, breaking off easily in storms. Its roots can get into underground pipes, and even its big seeds can be a nuisance when they litter the ground.

LEAVES GREEN ABOVE,
PALE BELOW, WITH FIVE
DEEP, POINTED LOBES

LONG SAMARAS
IN PAIRS IN SPRING,
GREEN OR RED

Laugh Out Loud!
What do embarrassed maples do in the fall?
They turn red and leave.

Sugar Maple

Acer saccharum HEIGHT **70–100 ft (21.5–30.5 m)** · SHAPE **Medium to tall, with a straight trunk and dense, curved crown** · LEAVES **Opposite, simple, 4–6 in (10–15 cm), with 5 lobes** · FLOWERS **Yellow-green clusters** · FRUITS **Samaras in pairs** · RANGE **Eastern Canada, U.S. Northeast to Midwest** · HABITAT **Woodlands, stream banks** · OTHER NAMES **Hard Maple, Sugartree**

Sugar Maples are famous for their brilliant colors in autumn and sugary sweet sap. In late winter, when nights are below freezing but days are milder, people tap into the trees and collect their sap drip by drip. Then they boil it down to make syrup or candy. It takes 40 gallons (151 L) of sap to make one gallon (3.8 L) of syrup. The Sugar Maple also has a fine wood used in furniture and musical instruments. Its leaf appears on the national flag of Canada.

MAPLE SUGAR CANDY

With an adult's help, you can make maple syrup candy in the snow, just like the pioneers did. Use only pure syrup, not blends. Ingredients:

- 1 cup pure maple syrup
- Ice pop sticks
- Clean snow or crushed ice on a baking sheet
- Small saucepan
- Candy thermometer

1. With an adult's help, carefully heat the syrup to boiling in the saucepan, stirring constantly. Ideally it should reach 235°F (113°C) on a candy thermometer. (Don't touch the syrup! It's burning hot!)
2. Have the adult pour the syrup into strips on the snow or ice.
3. Roll up the cooling syrup around the ice pop stick. When it's cool, enjoy!

WIDE, FIVE-LOBED LEAVES; GREEN ABOVE, PALE BELOW

SAMARAS IN PAIRS IN LATE SUMMER OR EARLY FALL

Norway Maple

Acer platanoides HEIGHT 40–70 ft (12–21.5 m)
SHAPE Small to medium size with a dense, rounded crown • LEAVES Opposite, simple, 5–7 in (12.5–18 cm), with 5 lobes • FLOWERS Small yellow clusters • FRUITS Samaras in pairs • RANGE Native to Europe; widespread in northeastern and northwestern United States and Canada • HABITAT Streams, woods, cities • OTHER NAME European Maple

Some trees with lots of leafy branches are known as "shade trees," and few are shadier than the Norway Maple. Its dense crown of leaves, turning yellow in autumn, casts a dark shadow on the ground. This easy-to-grow broadleaf was brought to North America from northern Europe, and it has done well here. In fact, it may be doing too well. Norway Maples are crowding out native trees in some woodlands.

WIDE, FIVE-LOBED LEAVES WITH MANY POINTS

SMALL YELLOW-GREEN FLOWERS

SAMARAS IN PAIRS, SET AT A WIDE ANGLE

EXPERT'S CIRCLE

DON'T BE FOOLED

The Norway Maple and the Sugar Maple (opposite) look alike. To tell the difference, snap the leaf stem. Norway Maples give off a milky sap. You can make syrup from the Norway Maple's sap, but it isn't as sweet as the Sugar Maple's syrup.

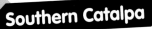

Southern Catalpa

Catalpa bignonioides HEIGHT 25–45 ft (7.5–13.5 m) · SHAPE Small to medium size with a wide or forked crown · LEAVES Opposite, simple, 5–12 in (12.5–30.5 cm), heart-shaped · FLOWERS Large white clusters · FRUITS Very long, slender seedpods · RANGE Eastern United States, particularly the South · HABITAT Streams, clearings · OTHER NAMES Indian Bean Tree, Cigar Tree, Catawba Tree, Fish Bait Tree

The Southern Catalpa is easy to spot. In late spring, showy white flowers bloom among its leaves. In summer and autumn, seeds hang from the tree in long, narrow pods that look like string beans. It is widely planted in mild and warm regions in the East, but not everyone likes it. Its flowers and seedpods drop messily across the ground, and its leaves are stinky when crushed.

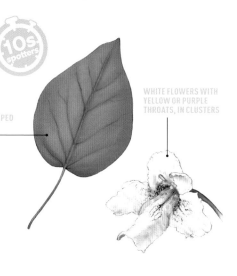

LARGE HEART-SHAPED LEAVES

WHITE FLOWERS WITH YELLOW OR PURPLE THROATS, IN CLUSTERS

NAME GAME

Fishermen know the Southern Catalpa as the Fish Bait Tree. The tree often hosts the larvae of the catalpa sphinx moth. This juicy caterpillar is a popular bait for fish, particularly bream.

Roughleaf Dogwood

Cornus drummondii HEIGHT 15–25 ft (4.5–7.5 m) · SHAPE Small, sometimes a shrub · LEAVES Opposite, simple, 2–4 in (5–10 cm), broadly heart-shaped · FLOWERS Small, in white clusters · FRUITS Hard white berries · RANGE Midwest, Great Plains, to Texas · HABITAT Shady woodlands · OTHER NAMES None

This pretty tree hovers on the borderline between tree and shrub. In some places, it has a single trunk and can be 25 feet (7.5 m) high. In others, it

GREEN, HEART-SHAPED LEAVES, ROUGH TO THE TOUCH

has many trunks and spreads out like a bush. Its white flowers are small and clustered, unlike those of its better-known cousin the Flowering Dogwood (see below). The leaves feel rough on their upper surfaces, giving the tree its common name. Birds like to eat its white berries, and they help spread the tree to new places.

Flowering Dogwood

Cornus florida HEIGHT 15–40 ft (4.5–12 m) · SHAPE Small, with short trunk and wide, spreading branches · LEAVES Opposite, simple, 2–6 in (5–15 cm), heart-shaped with pointed tip · FLOWERS Small and green, surrounded by large white or pink petal-like bracts · FRUITS Hard red berries · RANGE Eastern United States · HABITAT Shady woodlands on hillsides, at woodland edges, and along fences · OTHER NAMES None

The graceful Flowering Dogwood adds a touch of white-flowered beauty to woods and yards throughout the East. It's a small tree that grows well in shade. The large white (sometimes pink) "flowers" are actually bracts, a kind of leaf, that frame the little green flowers in the middle. Dogwoods are under threat from a disease called the anthracnose fungus, which can gradually kill the trees.

TINY YELLOW-GREEN FLOWERS SURROUNDED BY FOUR LARGE WHITE OR PINK BRACTS

BE A TREE HUGGER!

In 1912, Japan gave cherry trees to Washington, D.C., as a gift. In 2012, the United States returned the favor by sending 3,000 Flowering Dogwood saplings to Japan.

SHINY GREEN HEART-SHAPED LEAVES WITH A POINTED TIP

TINY GREEN FLOWERS SURROUNDED BY FOUR TO SEVEN LARGE WHITE OR PINK BRACTS

→ **LOOK FOR THIS** On all **DOG-WOODS,** the leaf veins follow the shape of the leaf edge: They curve out from the midrib and back toward the tip.

Pacific Dogwood

Cornus nuttallii HEIGHT 20–50 ft (6–15 m) · SHAPE Small, with a narrow crown in woods or wide crown in open spaces · LEAVES Opposite, simple, 3–6 in (7.5–15 cm), heart-shaped with pointed tip · FLOWERS Small and green, surrounded by large white or pink petal-like bracts · FRUITS Shiny red or orange berries · RANGE Pacific coast from Canada to California · HABITAT Mountain forests · OTHER NAMES None

The Pacific Dogwood is the West Coast cousin of the East Coast's Flowering Dogwood (see page 59). This attractive tree with pink or white blossoms is found mixed in with other trees, such as Douglas-firs (see page 48), in Pacific coastal forests. It blooms in spring and, often, again in early autumn. Like other dogwoods, it is threatened by the anthracnose fungus.

Empress Tree

LARGE HEART-SHAPED LEAVES, SLIGHTLY HAIRY

TUBE-SHAPED PURPLE FLOWERS IN CLUSTERS

Paulownia tomentosa HEIGHT 30–60 ft (9–18.5 m) · SHAPE Small to medium size, with short trunk and broad crown · LEAVES Opposite, simple, 5–14 in (12.5–35.5 cm), heart-shaped · FLOWERS Purple, tube-shaped, in clusters · FRUITS Brown, oval seed capsules · RANGE Native to China; widespread in eastern United States · HABITAT Vacant lots, gardens, and parks · OTHER NAMES Princess Tree, Royal Paulownia

The Empress Tree (genus *Paulownia*) was named by a Dutch scientist after Anna Pavlovna, queen of the Netherlands. It is native to China but has now been planted on every continent except Antarctica. This very fast-growing tree has beautiful, sweet-smelling purple flowers. Each of its seedpods holds thousands of fluffy winged seeds, and one tree can release 20 million seeds each year. Because of this, the Empress Tree has spread rapidly and has become an invasive species across much of the eastern United States.

Laugh Out Loud! How do you identify a dogwood tree? By its bark!

Red Mangrove

Rhizophora mangle HEIGHT 20–40 ft (6–12 m) · SHAPE Small, with irregular crown and visible arching roots · LEAVES Opposite, simple, 2–6 in (5–15 cm), slender oval · FLOWERS Small, pale yellow, in small clusters · FRUITS Reddish brown berries · RANGE Coastal South Florida and Texas · HABITAT Coastal waters, riverbanks · OTHER NAME American Mangrove

The amazing Red Mangrove is a unique tree of the American tropics. It grows right out of brackish (somewhat salty) waters on the coasts of Florida and Texas. Its roots sprout from high up on the tree trunk and arch through the air before entering the water. This way, they can collect oxygen from the open air. Mangrove seeds sprout while they are still on the tree. The seedlings grow down from the seeds like slender beans before dropping into the water, where they float away to find a new home.

SEEDLINGS SPROUT FROM REDDISH BROWN PODS.

SHINY, DARK GREEN, LEATHERY LEAVES

SMALL, PALE YELLOW FLOWERS

BE A TREE HUGGER!

Mangrove forests are an important part of the tropical ecosystem. Baby fish are born and take shelter there. Pelicans and egrets live in the trees and hunt for fish from the branches. And the tangled forests protect coastlines from high winds and waves during tropical storms.

Pawpaw

Asimina triloba HEIGHT 15–40 ft (4.5–12 m) · SHAPE Small, with straight or multistemmed trunk, wide crown · LEAVES Alternate, simple, 6–12 in (15–30.5 cm), long oval with pointed tip · FLOWERS Purple, bell-shaped · FRUITS Large, egg-shaped, fleshy · RANGE Southern Canada, eastern United States to Great Plains and Texas · HABITAT Moist woodlands, streams · OTHER NAMES Indian Banana, Custard Apple

The Pawpaw belongs to a family of trees known as custard apples. This small tree (sometimes a shrub) is known for its big, fleshy fruit. The fruit's sweet flesh tastes somewhat like bananas, and people and animals compete to eat it when it becomes ripe in autumn. However, the tree does not please everyone. Its purple flowers have a nasty smell, and some people are allergic to its fruit.

NAME GAME

The childlike name Pawpaw probably comes from "papaya," a tropical fruit that looks similar to the Pawpaw's but isn't related.

LONG, POINTED LEAVES

LARGE, FLESHY YELLOW OR BROWN FRUIT

PURPLE, BELL-SHAPED FLOWERS

American Holly

Ilex opaca HEIGHT 20–50 ft (6–15 m) SHAPE Small to medium size, cone-shaped crown LEAVES Alternate, simple, 2–4 in (5–10 cm), stiff and fleshy, with sharply toothed edge FLOWERS Tiny, pale green, in clusters FRUITS Small, red, berrylike RANGE East and southeast to Texas HABITAT Sandy coastal forests to mountains OTHER NAMES None

You see the shiny green leaves and bright red fruits of the American Holly everywhere during the holidays. The tree is a popular choice for yards. It can be as small as a shrub or tall and pointed. The American Holly comes in male and female forms. Only the female grows berries, but it needs a male plant nearby to do so. Deer and birds like to eat the berries, but these fruits can be poisonous to people and pets—so don't try them yourself!

BE A TREE HUGGER!

American Hollies are broadleaf trees, but also evergreen. They hold on to their leaves all winter.

RED BERRYLIKE FRUITS IN CLUSTERS ON FEMALE TREES

STIFF, SHINY GREEN LEAVES WITH POINTY, TOOTHED EDGES

Red Alder

Alnus rubra HEIGHT 20–80 ft (6–24.5 m) · SHAPE Small to medium size with cone-shaped crown · LEAVES Alternate, simple, 3–6 in (7.5–15 cm), oval, pointed, with toothed edges · FLOWERS Long, orange-yellow catkins · FRUITS Small, in cone-shaped clusters · RANGE Pacific coast from Alaska to California · HABITAT Woodlands, stream banks, clear-cut open spaces · OTHER NAMES Pacific Coast Alder, Western Alder

The straight, slender Red Alder grows fast—about three feet (1 m) a year—in woods and clearings. Native Americans used to make a red dye from its reddish inner bark. When they stained their fishing nets with the dye, the nets were hard for the fish to see in dark waters. Red Alders grow well in open spaces. Their leaves, falling on the ground, make the soil richer when they decay. That's why people often plant them in clear-cut areas when they want to grow new woodlands.

NAME GAME

What's a catkin, and what's it doing on a tree? Catkins are slim groups of flowers that grow from many kinds of trees, such as birches and willows. They take their name from the Old Dutch word *katteken*, which means "kitten," because they look like a kitten's tail.

OVAL, POINTED LEAVES WITH TOOTHED EDGES; DARK GREEN ABOVE, GRAY-GREEN BELOW

LONG, YELLOW-GREEN CATKINS

FRUITS IN CONELIKE CLUSTERS

Hazel Alder

Alnus serrulata   HEIGHT **15–20 ft (4.5–6 m)**
· SHAPE **Small, thin, sometimes with many stems**
· LEAVES **Alternate, simple, 2–5 in (5–12.5 cm),
oval, pointed** · FLOWERS **Catkins, hanging or
upright** · FRUITS **Small, woody, cone-shaped**
· RANGE **Eastern Canada, eastern United States
west to Oklahoma** · HABITAT **Stream banks,
swamps** · OTHER NAME **Smooth Alder**

Look for the Hazel Alder
near streams and in
swamps—it likes wet places.
This skinny broadleaf tree can
be as small as a shrub, sometimes growing in tangled groups.
Its long roots help hold soil in place
along stream banks. Hazel Alders give shelter
to many animals, including a fat little bird, the
American woodcock.

BE A TREE HUGGER!

Native Americans used to
make a tea from Hazel Alder
bark. They drank it to ease
the pain of toothaches and
other ailments.

FLOWERS IN
CATKINS, DANGLING
OR UPRIGHT

OVAL, POINTED
LEAVES WITH
WAVY EDGES

FRUITS
IN SMALL,
CONE-SHAPED
CLUSTERS

American Hornbeam

Carpinus caroliniana HEIGHT **20–35 ft (6–10.5 m)**
· SHAPE **Small, with a rounded, broad crown** · LEAVES
Alternate, simple, 2–4 in (5–10 cm), slender pointed oval
· FLOWERS **Short catkins** · FRUITS **Small, green, nutlike,
surrounded by green leafy bracts** · RANGE **Eastern and
midwestern United States to Texas** · HABITAT **Low
forests, stream banks** · OTHER NAMES **Musclewood,
Ironwood, Blue Beech**

The American Hornbeam's
common names tell you a lot
about the tree. It's called
"hornbeam" because its wood
can be polished until it's shiny,
like an animal horn. It's called
"musclewood" because its trunk and
branches are twisted and ropy, like a weight
lifter's muscles. And it's called "ironwood"
because its wood is super hard. People make
tools, bowls, and dishes out of it. The American
Hornbeam is a good-looking tree, about as
broad as it is tall.

→ LOOK FOR THIS
In late summer and autumn,
look for the **AMERICAN
HORNBEAM'S** little green
fruits. They sit inside winglike
green bracts (leafy structures)
that dangle from the tree
in clusters.

FLOWERS IN CATKINS

OVAL, POINTED,
DARK GREEN LEAVES

NUTLIKE FRUITS
IN THREE-LEAFED
GREEN BRACTS

Yellow Birch

Betula alleghaniensis HEIGHT 50–75 ft (15–23 m) · SHAPE Medium to tall, with a straight trunk and narrow, rounded crown · LEAVES Alternate, simple, 3–5 in (7.5–12.5 cm), pointed oval · FLOWERS Hanging or upright catkins · FRUITS Small, upright, in cone-shaped clusters · RANGE Southeastern Canada, northeastern United States to Great Lakes and Georgia · HABITAT Cool forests, mountain slopes, stream banks · OTHER NAMES Swamp Birch, Gray Birch, Silver Birch

You'll find the Yellow Birch mixed in with other trees in northeastern forests. Look for its golden bark and, in autumn, golden leaves. The shiny bark peels off in strips that circle around the tree. It's a long-lived tree, and in old forests, some Yellow Birches may be as much as 300 years old. Its strong wood is often used in furniture, houses, and tools.

OVAL, POINTED LEAVES WITH FINELY TOOTHED EDGES

→ LOOK FOR THIS
Scratch a **YELLOW BIRCH** twig and you'll smell a sharp, minty, wintergreen odor. It's just like the smell of some chewing gums or hard candies.

River Birch

Betula nigra HEIGHT 50–70 ft (15–21.5 m) · SHAPE Medium to tall, sometimes with many trunks, broad crown · LEAVES Alternate, simple, 1.5–3 in (4–7.5 cm), triangular · FLOWERS Hanging or upright catkins · FRUITS Small, upright, in cone-shaped clusters · RANGE New England west to Minnesota, south to northern Florida and west to Texas · HABITAT Stream banks, swamps · OTHER NAME Red Birch

TRIANGULAR LEAVES, SHARPLY TOOTHED

PEELING, REDDISH BARK

The fast-growing River Birch likes the water. You'll often find it around streams or swamps, but people like to plant it in yards and along streets because of its pretty broad and branching shape. Its rust-colored bark peels back to show smooth, pinkish wood underneath. The River Birch's catkins appear in early spring, before its leaves come out. By summer, the tree has already grown its seeds, held inside little brown conelike clusters.

Water Birch

Betula occidentalis HEIGHT 20–35 ft (6–10.5 m)
· SHAPE Small, sometimes shrublike, often with many
stems, irregular crown · LEAVES Alternate, simple, 0.75–
2 in (2–5 cm), rounded or wedge-shaped · FLOWERS Small
hanging or upright catkins · FRUITS Small, drooping, in
slender conelike clusters · RANGE Western United States,
particularly Rocky Mountains · HABITAT Stream banks,
woods · OTHER NAMES Rocky Mountain Birch, Black Birch

The little Water Birch grows along
streams and lakes in the West. Its
bark is shiny and red to dark gray.
Unlike the bark of many other birches,
it doesn't peel off. The tree's roots help to
hold soil in place along stream banks. The Water
Birch is very important for wildlife. Its leaves
feed goats, mule deer, and elk, while beavers use
the branches to build their dams.

SMALL OVAL LEAVES
WITH POINTED TIP,
TOOTHED EDGES

YELLOW-GREEN
CATKINS

Laugh Out Loud!

What did the beaver say
to the Water Birch?

It's been nice gnawing you!

Paper Birch

Betula papyrifera HEIGHT 50-70 ft (15-21.5 m)
• SHAPE Medium size, with one or more slender trunks, irregular crown • LEAVES Alternate, simple, 2-3 in (5-7.5 cm), oval, pointed
• FLOWERS Pale green or yellowish catkins
• FRUITS Slender, drooping cone-shaped clusters • RANGE Canada and northern United States from coast to coast • HABITAT Cool, sunny areas with moist soil • OTHER NAME White Birch

With its bright white bark, dotted with dark spots, the Paper Birch is an easy tree to recognize. It grows in cold northern regions across North America, from the Atlantic to the Pacific. The Paper Birch is a pioneer species. That means that it is among the first trees to grow again in places that have been burned by wildfires. Native Americans, such as the Anishinabe, have long used the Paper Birch's waterproof bark to make baskets, houses, and canoes.

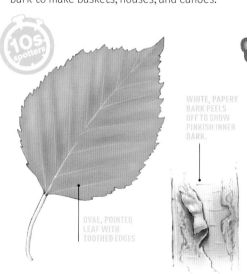

WHITE, PAPERY BARK PEELS OFF TO SHOW PINKISH INNER BARK.

OVAL, POINTED LEAF WITH TOOTHED EDGES

BE A TREE HUGGER!

The Anishinabe people of the Great Lakes area have several legends about the Paper Birch. In one story, the hero Manabozho stole fire from a thunderbird's nest. When the great bird chased him, he hid in a hollow birch tree. The thunderbird blasted the tree with lightning, but it couldn't hurt Manabozho. To this day, all Paper Birches bear the black scars of the thunderbird's lightning strikes.

TREE-MENDOUS: THE COLORS OF AUTUMN

Green

In summer, leaves make food for their trees using sunlight, carbon dioxide gas, and a chemical called chlorophyll. Chlorophyll is green, so leaves are green.

TREES WITH BRIGHTLY COLORED AUTUMN LEAVES LINE A WINDING TRAIL IN NEW ENGLAND.

In autumn, nature puts on a party. On most broadleaf trees, leaves turn bright yellow, orange, red, or purple. The color change begins as the days become shorter and trees get less sunlight. As the days stay warm and the nights grow colder, the colors become more vibrant. Here's what happens to make each color.

Yellow and Orange

In autumn, leaves get less sunlight. They can't make enough food for their trees. Their chlorophyll goes away. But leaves have other colors that are covered up by green chlorophyll. As the green fades, natural yellow and orange colors show up in the leaves.

Red

Some trees make a new color—bright red—in their leaves in autumn. Tree scientists aren't sure what that red color is for. It might protect the leaves while they're sending food to the tree. It definitely makes the trees beautiful.

Red-Yellow-Orange-Purple

A few trees have it all: red, yellow, orange, and purple leaves on one tree. The different colors depend on the climate and also how the leaf pigments change in the fall.

Virginia Roundleaf Birch

Betula uber HEIGHT To 40 ft (12 m) · SHAPE Small to medium size, oval crown · LEAVES Alternate, simple, 1.5–2.5 in (4–6.5 cm), oval or rounded · FLOWERS Small catkins · FRUITS Tiny samaras · RANGE Southwestern Virginia · HABITAT Stream banks · OTHER NAME Ashe's Birch

We know that rare animals are put on the endangered species list when they are close to becoming extinct. Trees can also be endangered. The Virginia Roundleaf Birch is one of them. In 1918, scientists discovered a few of these little birches growing along one creek in southwestern Virginia. Then they couldn't find them again and thought the tree was extinct. In the 1970s, scientists rediscovered them and began growing more in protected areas. These trees are still considered critically endangered. Because of their special pollinating process, it is hard for them to reproduce. Only a handful remain along the original creek. If you spot one, you're looking at a tree few humans have ever seen!

BE A TREE HUGGER!

The Virginia Roundleaf Birch was the first tree ever to be protected by the Endangered Species Act.

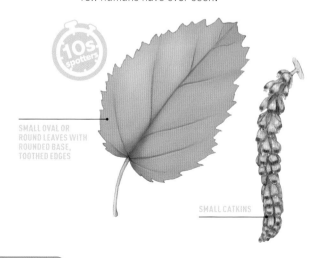

SMALL OVAL OR ROUND LEAVES WITH ROUNDED BASE, TOOTHED EDGES

SMALL CATKINS

Common Persimmon

Diospyros virginiana HEIGHT 30–40 ft (9–12 m) · SHAPE Small, with a short trunk and low, round crown · LEAVES Alternate, simple, 2.5–6 in (6.5–15 cm), slender oval · FLOWERS Small, white or purple, bell-shaped · FRUITS Fleshy, round · RANGE East and south, Connecticut to Texas · HABITAT River bottoms, woods · OTHER NAMES Possumwood, American Ebony

Common Persimmons are small, mostly southern trees with dark brown or gray bark. They are best known for their round fruits, only an inch or two (2.5–5 cm) wide, which hang on to the branches of female trees after the leaves have fallen. If eaten before they are ripe, the fruits are mouth-puckeringly bitter. When they are very ripe, they are soft and sweet. The ripe fruit is good eaten fresh or baked into pies, jams, or other treats.

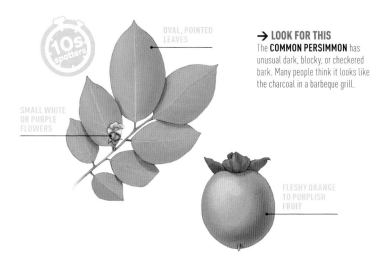

10s spotters

OVAL, POINTED LEAVES

SMALL WHITE OR PURPLE FLOWERS

→ **LOOK FOR THIS**
The **COMMON PERSIMMON** has unusual dark, blocky, or checkered bark. Many people think it looks like the charcoal in a barbeque grill.

FLESHY ORANGE TO PURPLISH FRUIT

Sourwood

Oxydendrum arboreum HEIGHT 40–60 ft (12–18.5 m) · SHAPE Small to medium size, slender trunk, branches sometimes drooping to the ground · LEAVES Alternate, simple, 5–8 in (12.5–20.5 cm), slender pointed oval · FLOWERS Small, white, in long clusters · FRUITS Silver-gray cups holding tiny seeds · RANGE Southeast from Pennsylvania to Florida · HABITAT Shady woods, yards · OTHER NAMES Lily-of-the-Valley Tree, Sorrel Tree

The Sourwood's leaves (but not its wood) are certainly sour. Even so, the tree is planted over a wide area because it's a lovely sight spring through winter. Dangling white flower clusters hang from the trees in spring. In autumn, Sourwood leaves turn a brilliant, glowing red. When the leaves have fallen, the silvery little seed cups hang from the twigs for a while.

TRY THIS!

MAKE A LEAF ALBUM
Make a book of leaves you've collected. Here's what you need:
• A roll of wax paper
• Heavy books
• An empty album
• Leaves

1. Collect the leaves you like. Make sure they are smooth and without spots or rips.
2. Put two pieces of wax paper facing each other inside an open heavy book (with an adult's permission). Slip the leaf between the papers and close the book. Pile books on top.
3. In two weeks, open up the book. The leaf should be flat and dry.
4. Label it with the tree's name and the date and place you found it.
5. Place it and its label under the plastic cover of an album page.
6. Repeat with different leaves.

SLENDER, OVAL, POINTED LEAVES

LONG WHITE FLOWER CLUSTERS

10s spotters

LEAVES TURN BRIGHT RED IN AUTUMN

BE A TREE HUGGER!

Bees make a sweet-smelling, rich honey from Sourwood flowers.

Crape Myrtle

Lagerstroemia indica HEIGHT 15–30 ft (4.5–9 m) · SHAPE Small, sometimes with many stems, vase-shaped crown · LEAVES Alternate, simple, 1.5–3 in (4–7.5 cm), slender pointed oval · FLOWERS White, pink, purple, or red in large clusters · FRUITS Oval capsules, green to brown · RANGE Native to Asia; U.S. East through South · HABITAT Streets and yards · OTHER NAME Lilac of the South

The Crape Myrtle is a favorite tree for yards and streets. It was brought into the United States from Asia, and now it can be found throughout the East and South. This flowering tree really packs on the buds. In summer, big clusters of white, pink, red, or purple flowers bloom on the ends of its twigs. These flowers may last for months. In winter, the tree's smooth, colorful bark and its twisted shape keep it looking interesting even without flowers.

OVAL LEAVES WITH SMOOTH EDGES

BIG FLOWER CLUSTERS ON ENDS OF TWIGS

NAME GAME

Crape Myrtles are named for their flowers, which are crinkled like crepe paper. (Sometimes the tree's name is spelled Crepe Myrtle.) The Japanese call it the Monkey Slip Tree because its bark is so smooth that monkeys slip on it.

Eastern Redbud

Cercis canadensis HEIGHT 15–30 ft (4.5–9 m) · SHAPE Small, sometimes with many trunks, broad crown · LEAVES Alternate, simple, 5–8 in (12.5–20.5 cm), heart-shaped · FLOWERS Purplish pink, sometimes white, in clusters · FRUITS Flat, narrow pods · RANGE Eastern United States · HABITAT Moist woods, valleys; yards · OTHER NAME Judas Tree

The glowing pink flowers of the Eastern Redbud bring a splash of color to woods and yards in early spring. Flower clusters grow not only from the tree's branches but also from its trunk. Later, broad, heart-shaped leaves appear, then dangling flat seedpods. The Eastern Redbud grows easily in many places. You'll see it throughout the eastern United States.

CLUSTERS OF WHITE OR PINK FLOWERS ON BRANCHES AND TRUNK

EXPERT'S CIRCLE

DON'T BE FOOLED Unlike all the other trees in this section, the Eastern Redbud is a member of the pea *(Fabaceae)* family. Look closely, and you'll see that its flowers look like pea flowers, and its seedpods look like peapods.

American Beech

Fagus grandifolia HEIGHT 65–80 ft (20–24.5 m) · SHAPE Tall, with stout branches and dense crown · LEAVES Alternate, simple, 3–5 in (7.5–12.5 cm), pointed oval · FLOWERS Small, greenish clusters · FRUITS 1–3 nuts in prickly husk · RANGE Eastern Canada, eastern United States and Great Lakes · HABITAT Mixed forests, hillsides · OTHER NAMES Carolina Beech, Gray Beech

The tall, slow-growing American Beech can be found in many eastern forests. With its smooth, gray bark and thick branches, it is easy to spot. Many animals, including squirrels, chipmunks, black bears, deer, and turkeys, eat the tasty beech nuts, which ripen inside four-sided husks in autumn. People don't usually eat the nuts, but sometimes they roast them and make them into a kind of coffee.

OVAL, POINTED, DARK GREEN LEAVES WITH TOOTHED EDGES

American Chestnut

Castanea dentata HEIGHT **10–100 ft (3–30.5 m)**
· SHAPE **Old trees: tall, with big trunk and broad crown; young trees: short, slender, with narrow crown** · LEAVES **Alternate, simple, 6–10 in (15–25.5 cm), narrow pointed oval** · FLOWERS **Pale yellow catkins** · FRUITS **Round, prickly husks around large seed** · RANGE **Eastern United States, scattered in Midwest and West** · HABITAT **Forests and mountain slopes** · OTHER NAMES **None**

"Under a spreading chestnut-tree" are the first words of a famous poem by H. W. Longfellow. Longfellow was writing in the 19th century, when huge chestnut trees were common. One out of every four trees in the East was an American Chestnut. Now those trees are almost extinct. Around 1900, Asian Chestnut trees that were brought into the United States carried with them a disease called chestnut blight. It spread quickly through American Chestnuts and killed almost all of them within 40 years. Today, a few big trees can be found in the West. In the East, you can still see small young American Chestnut trees. They sprout up from old stumps, but they usually die within a few years. Plant scientists are trying to breed trees that will fight the disease.

LONG, NARROW, POINTED LEAVES WITH SHARPLY TOOTHED EDGES

SHINY BROWN NUTS INSIDE SPINY HUSKS

BE A TREE HUGGER!

The biggest American Chestnuts were as tall as a seven-story building and as wide as a small bedroom. Some old chestnuts in open areas grew as tall as they grew wide. One remaining national champion measures 70 feet by 70 feet (21.5 m by 21.5 m)!

White Oak

Quercus alba HEIGHT **50–80 ft (15–24.5 m)** • SHAPE **Medium to tall, with wide, irregular crown** • LEAVES **Alternate, simple, 5–7 in (12.5–18 cm), deeply lobed, with smooth, rounded edges** • FLOWERS **Hanging green catkins** • FRUITS **Acorns** • RANGE **Eastern United States** • HABITAT **Widespread in woods and yards** • OTHER NAME **Eastern White Oak**

If you live in the eastern United States, you've probably seen plenty of White Oaks. These tall and wide-spreading trees with shaggy gray bark are among the most common trees in the country. White Oaks are prized for their wood, which is often used for floors and woodwork in houses. Animals such as squirrels and blue jays like them for their tasty acorns, which ripen at the end of one season, which lasts a year. Creatures snatch them from the ground and store them in hiding places. White Oaks can live up to 600 years and grow as tall as 100 feet (30.5 m).

→ LOOK FOR THIS

Most oaks are divided into two groups: **RED OAKS** and **WHITE OAKS**. Red oaks have reddish wood, and white oak wood is creamy white.

Red oaks have the following:
- Leaves with pointed lobes and sharp bristles on their tips
- Flat scales on the acorn cup
- Dark, smooth, or ridged bark

White oaks have the following:
- Leaves usually with rounded, smooth lobes
- Bumpy scales on the acorn cup
- Paler, scaly bark

LEAVES WITH MEDIUM TO DEEP LOBES, SMOOTH ROUNDED EDGES

CUP COVERS ONE-THIRD OF LIGHT BROWN ACORN.

Arizona White Oak

Quercus arizonica HEIGHT 30–60 ft (9–18.5 m) • SHAPE Small to medium size, with short trunk and wide crown • LEAVES Alternate, simple, 1–3 in (2.5–7.5 cm), narrow ovals with a few teeth along edges • FLOWERS Catkins • FRUITS Acorns • RANGE Central Arizona, New Mexico to Texas • HABITAT Woods, canyons, grasslands • OTHER NAME Arizona Oak

SMALL, NARROW, FLESHY LEAVES

A sturdy tree, the Arizona White Oak has a short trunk and thick, twisted branches. You'll find this white oak in the woods and grasslands of the American Southwest. Its leaves are not lobed, like those of many oaks, but instead are narrow ovals. These thick leaves are almost evergreen: They stay on the branches until spring, when new leaves start to grow. It takes one year for the acorns to ripen. Animals don't usually eat the acorns, but white-tailed deer and mule deer like to munch on the branches.

EXPERT'S CIRCLE

DON'T BE FOOLED Oaks, which are part of the beech family that includes the American Beech (see page 76), grow almost everywhere. Ninety species live in the United States. They come in different shapes and sizes, but one thing is always the same: If it has an acorn, it's an oak!

Scarlet Oak

Quercus coccinea HEIGHT 60–80 ft (18.5–24.5 m) • SHAPE Medium size, with open, rounded crown • LEAVES Alternate, simple, 3–7 in (7.5–18 cm), deeply lobed • FLOWERS Catkins • FRUITS Acorns • RANGE Eastern and central United States • HABITAT Forests, slopes; yards • OTHER NAMES Black Oak, Spanish Oak

LEAVES HAVE SEVEN TO NINE DEEP LOBES WITH POINTED TIPS.

Scarlet Oaks blaze bright red in autumn all over the eastern and central United States. In spring, their new leaves are also red, changing to a shiny green in summer. Scarlet Oaks belong to the red oak group, and their leaves have the classic pointy tips of that group of trees. Young Scarlet Oaks have smooth gray bark. In older trees, the bark turns darker and rougher.

Southern Red Oak

Quercus falcata HEIGHT 60–80 ft (18.5–24.5 m) · SHAPE Medium size, straight trunk, round crown · LEAVES Alternate, simple, 4–9 in (10–23 cm), lobed · FLOWERS Catkins · FRUITS Acorns · RANGE Southeast to southern Missouri, eastern Texas · HABITAT Dry, sunny uplands · OTHER NAME Spanish Oak

LEAVES WITH THREE TO FIVE DEEP LOBES, POINTED AT TIPS

With its straight trunk and round, open crown, the Southern Red Oak is a handsome tree. It likes warm temperatures and dry, sandy soils. Its leaves, dark green on top and pale green and hairy on the underside, have a rounded base that looks a little like a duck's foot. Young trees have smooth bark, but in older trees the bark grows dark and ridged. Like many other red oaks, the Southern Red Oak has strong, light-red wood that is used in furniture and cabinets.

Oregon White Oak

Quercus garryana HEIGHT 25–90 ft (7.5–27.5 m) · SHAPE Small to tall, short trunk, wide crown · LEAVES Alternate, simple, 3–4 in (7.5–10 cm), lobed · FLOWERS Catkins · FRUITS Acorns · RANGE Western Canada to central California · HABITAT Woods, hillsides · OTHER NAMES Garry Oak, Oregon Oak

LEAVES WITH FIVE TO NINE ROUNDED LOBES, GROWING WIDER TOWARD THE TIP

Oregon White Oaks are the only native oak trees that grow in the U.S. Northwest. They vary a lot in size. In dry, warm areas, they may be as small as shrubs. In cool northern places, they are tall trees. Oregon White Oaks grow best in regions where fires sweep through the grass. That's because fires kill Douglas-firs. Without fires, Douglas-firs grow taller than Oregon White Oaks and block off their sunlight, and the oaks can't survive.

→ **LOOK FOR THIS** Sometimes you'll see round swellings on oak leaves or twigs. These are called galls. They appear when insects, such as gall wasps, lay eggs in the leaves. The galls look as if they might be harmful, but they don't usually hurt the leaves.

Gambel Oak

Quercus gambelii HEIGHT **10–30 ft (3–9 m)**
· SHAPE **Small, sometimes shrublike, narrow crown**
· LEAVES **Alternate, simple, 3–6 in (7.5–15 cm), lobed**
· FLOWERS **Catkins** · FRUITS **Acorns** · RANGE **Utah,
Wyoming, Arizona, New Mexico** · HABITAT **Dry
areas in foothills and on mountain slopes**
· OTHER NAMES **Rocky Mountain White Oak,
Utah White Oak**

The little Gambel Oak is
common in the southern
Rocky Mountains, growing
along with Ponderosa Pines
on hills and mountain slopes.
Its wood is not good for making
furniture, but it makes fine firewood.
Animals and insects love the Gambel Oak.
Pigeons, turkeys, and squirrels eat the acorns. Deer graze on the leaves.
Rare Mexican spotted owls nest in the branches. The Colorado hairstreak
butterfly depends on this oak completely. Its caterpillars eat only
Gambel Oak leaves when they come out in the spring.

YELLOW-GREEN
LEAVES WITH
FIVE TO NINE
DEEP, ROUNDED
LOBES

CAP COVERS ONE-THIRD OF OVAL
ACORN, WHICH IS GREEN WHEN YOUNG
AND LIGHT BROWN WHEN RIPE.

NAME GAME

The Gambel Oak is
named after a young 19th-
century scientist, William
Gambel. At the age of 18
he set out into the Wild
West to collect plants,
birds, and other wildlife.
He discovered many new
species, including
Gambel's quail, which is
also named after him. He
was only 26 years old in
1849 when he died of
typhoid, after stopping
to help a group of sick
gold miners.

California Live Oak

Quercus agrifolia HEIGHT 30–80 ft (9–24.5 m) · SHAPE Small to tall; short, crooked trunk, sometimes many trunks; broad crown · LEAVES Alternate, simple, 1–3 in (2.5–7.5 cm), oval · FLOWERS Catkins · FRUITS Acorns · RANGE California coast · HABITAT Woodlands, valleys, slopes · OTHER NAME Coast Live Oak

SMALL OVAL LEAVES WITH BRISTLY TEETH AROUND EDGES

The California Live Oak, with its wide, drooping crown of small leaves, is a common sight along the California coast. The tree grows well in the region's mild winters and hot summers. Many animals live in California Live Oak woods, including black bears, black-tailed deer, wild pigs, and acorn woodpeckers. Red-shouldered hawks hunt among the trees. The tree doesn't mind fires. New trees will grow from the base of lightly burned trunks.

NAME GAME

Why is this called a "live" oak? Aren't all living oaks "live"? Yes, they are, but live oaks are named for their leaves, which don't die in winter. The California Live Oak and other live oaks are evergreens.

Shingle Oak

Quercus imbricaria HEIGHT 40–60 ft (12–18.5 m) · SHAPE Medium size, cone-shaped crown · LEAVES Alternate, simple, 4–6 in (10–15 cm), oval · FLOWERS Catkins · FRUITS Acorns · RANGE Midwest and upper South · HABITAT Sunny hillsides, valleys · OTHER NAME Northern Laurel Oak

LONG, OVAL, POINTED LEAVES WITH BRISTLY TIP; DARK GREEN ABOVE, SOFT AND HAIRY UNDERNEATH

Shingle Oaks live throughout the hills and valleys of the Midwest, especially in the Ohio River Valley. People used to make roof shingles from their wood, giving them their common name. Shingle Oak leaves are different from those of most oak trees. They are long, oval, pointed, and smooth, with no lobes or teeth along the edges. The trees aren't evergreen, but their leaves often hang on well into the winter.

Valley Oak

Quercus lobata HEIGHT 40–60 ft (12–18.5 m)
· SHAPE **Small to tall, wide trunk, broad crown**
· LEAVES **Alternate, simple, 2–4 in (5–10 cm),
lobed** · FLOWERS **Catkins** · FRUITS **Acorns**
· RANGE **Inland California** · HABITAT
Grasslands, low hills, valleys · OTHER NAME
California White Oak

These California oak trees are small when they grow in the salty air near the coast. Farther inland, they are taller, have wider bodies, and look very impressive. Eighteenth-century English explorer George Vancouver called them "stately lords of the forest." Valley Oaks can live to be hundreds of years old. As they age, the ends of the trees' broad branches may droop toward the ground. Many Valley Oaks were cut down in the 20th century as farms expanded in California. Now, foresters are trying to replant the trees in developed areas.

TREE TOPPERS!

The Henley Oak in Mendocino County, California, may be the tallest oak in North America. This Valley Oak is 151 feet (46 m) tall. That's as tall as the Statue of Liberty from its base to its torch. The tree is more than 500 years old.

SMALL LEAVES
WITH 9 TO 11
DEEP, ROUNDED
LOBES

NARROW,
POINTED
ACORN

Bur Oak

Quercus macrocarpa **HEIGHT 50–100 ft (15–30.5 m)** · **SHAPE Medium to tall, tall trunk, wide crown** · **LEAVES Alternate, simple, 6–12 in (15–30.5 cm), lobed** · **FLOWERS Catkins** · **FRUITS Acorns** · **RANGE South-central Canada through eastern and midwestern United States** · **HABITAT Damp woods, grasslands, rocky hillsides** · **OTHER NAMES Mossycup Oak, Blue Oak**

Bur Oaks are impressive: They're tall and strong, with big trunks and wide crowns. They once grew widely across eastern prairies. As towns and cities spread, most of these trees were cut down. Even so, they can still be found in many areas, from woods to city streets. Bur Oaks have the largest acorns of any oak. The acorn's cap covers most of the nut and ends in a fluffy fringe.

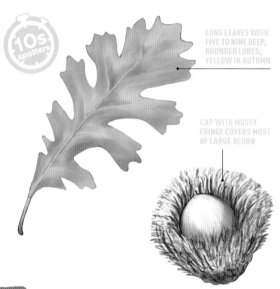

LONG LEAVES WITH FIVE TO NINE DEEP, ROUNDED LOBES; YELLOW IN AUTUMN

CAP WITH MOSSY FRINGE COVERS MOST OF LARGE ACORN

NAME GAME

The Bur Oak's species name, *macrocarpa*, means "big seed." Another of its common names, Mossycup Oak, refers to the acorn as well, with its mossy fringed cap.

Overcup Oak

Quercus lyrata HEIGHT **60–80 ft (18.5–24.5 m)** • SHAPE **Medium size, short trunk, irregular crown** • LEAVES **Alternate, simple, 6–10 in (15–25.5 cm), lobed** • FLOWERS **Catkins** • FRUITS **Acorns** • RANGE **Deep South and Mississippi Valley** • HABITAT **Swamps, stream banks** • OTHER NAMES **Swamp Post Oak, Water White Oak**

Overcup Oaks like warm, wet places. You'll find these slow-growing trees on the edges of swamps and in places that are often flooded. They get their common name from their odd acorns, which are covered almost completely by their caps. The acorns' spongy shells help them float around and take root in new spots in the Overcup Oak's watery habitat.

LEAVES WITH 5 TO 11 ROUNDED LOBES, NARROW BASE; DARK GREEN ABOVE, WHITISH UNDERNEATH

Cherrybark Oak

Quercus pagoda HEIGHT **70–100 ft (21.5–30.5 m)** • SHAPE **Medium to tall, tall trunk, high crown** • LEAVES **Alternate, simple, 5–8 in (12.5–20.5 cm), lobed** • FLOWERS **Catkins** • FRUITS **Acorns** • RANGE **Southeastern United States, Mississippi Valley** • HABITAT **Lowlands, riverbanks** • OTHER NAMES **Swamp Red Oak, Swamp Spanish Oak, Pagoda Oak**

SHINY GREEN LEAVES WITH 5 TO 11 LOBES; WHITISH AND HAIRY UNDERNEATH

The straight trunk of the Cherrybark Oak reaches up and up to a high crown of leaves. This tree of the warm and humid South has strong wood that is often used to make furniture and flooring. The Cherrybark Oak is named for its scaly, reddish bark, which looks like that of the Black Cherry tree. Squirrels, turkeys, blue jays, ducks, woodpeckers, and other animals feed on the tasty acorns.

Pin Oak

Quercus palustris HEIGHT **70–90 ft (21.5–27.5 m)** • SHAPE **Medium to tall; thick, cone-shaped crown** • LEAVES **Alternate, simple, 3–6 in (7.5–15 cm), lobed** • FLOWERS **Catkins** • FRUITS **Acorns** • RANGE **Mid-Atlantic and central states** • HABITAT **Wet flatlands, floodplains** • OTHER NAMES **Swamp Oak, Water Oak (Don't confuse it with another oak, *Quercus nigra*, which also has the common name Water Oak.)**

The Pin Oak may be named for dead branches that look like pins sticking out of its trunk. It is known not only for these branches but also for its overall shape. In a full-grown tree, the upper branches stick up toward the sky. The middle branches stick straight out to the sides, and the lower branches droop toward the ground. Pin Oaks grow well in wetlands, but they can be found in yards and along streets as well. In autumn, their leaves turn bright red, like those of the Scarlet Oak. Deer eat their seedlings, and ducks and turkeys enjoy the acorns.

EXPERT'S CIRCLE

DON'T BE FOOLED

Pin Oaks and Scarlet Oaks look alike. However, Pin Oak acorns have a small, shallow cap. Scarlet Oak acorns have a deep cap.

SHINY DARK GREEN LEAVES WITH FIVE TO NINE VERY DEEP LOBES

ROUND ACORN WITH SHALLOW CAP

Willow Oak

Quercus phellos HEIGHT **60–100 ft (18.5–30.5 m)**
· SHAPE **Medium to tall, tall trunk, rounded crown**
· LEAVES **Alternate, simple, 2–6 in (5–15 cm), narrow oval** · FLOWERS **Catkins** · FRUITS **Acorns** · RANGE **Mid-Atlantic to Texas** · HABITAT **Stream banks, woodlands**
· OTHER NAMES **Peach Oak, Swamp Willow Oak**

Willow Oaks grow in wet, flat areas, but people also like to plant them in yards and on streets. Their leaves are smooth and narrow, like those of willow trees. In the spring, the leaves are yellow-green. In summer, they turn a darker green, and then they may turn yellow, red, or orange in autumn.
Willow Oaks are important to all kinds of animals. Squirrels, ducks, deer, and turkeys eat the acorns. Flying squirrels live in the branches, and some butterflies lay their eggs among the leaves.

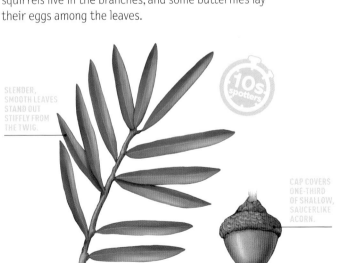

SLENDER, SMOOTH LEAVES STAND OUT STIFFLY FROM THE TWIG.

CAP COVERS ONE-THIRD OF SHALLOW, SAUCERLIKE ACORN.

Northern Red Oak

Quercus rubra HEIGHT 60–100 ft (18.5–30.5 m) · SHAPE Medium to tall, tall trunk, broad crown · LEAVES Alternate, simple, 4–9 in (10–23 cm), lobed · FLOWERS Catkins · FRUITS Acorns · RANGE Southeastern Canada, eastern United States · HABITAT Woods, slopes, valleys · OTHER NAMES Red Oak, Common Red Oak

You'll find this fast-growing tree all over the eastern United States. It has many uses. People plant it as a shade tree in yards and in parks. Builders use its strong wood to make everything from cabinets to railroad ties. Deer, moose, and rabbits eat its leaves, and Native Americans used to eat the acorns—though they had to boil or soak them in water to get rid of the bitter taste. Foresters often plant Northern Red Oaks to bring new life to old mining areas.

DULL GREEN LEAVES WITH 7 TO 11 POINTED LOBES

ACORNS CAN GROW TO 1.5 INCHES (4 CM) LONG.

Shumard Oak

Quercus shumardii HEIGHT 60–80 ft (18.5–24.5 m) · SHAPE Medium to tall; tall trunk; open, broad crown · LEAVES Alternate, simple, 6–8 in (15–20.5 cm), lobed · FLOWERS Catkins · FRUITS Acorns · RANGE Southeastern and central United States · HABITAT Wet woodlands, riverbanks · OTHER NAMES Swamp Red Oak, Shumard Red Oak, Southern Red Oak

The tall Shumard Oak, with its wide-spreading crown of leaves, is often planted as a shade tree. It's a tough tree that can survive dry spells or air pollution. In autumn, its wide leaves turn a bright red or orange. The Shumard Oak produces big crops of acorns, which feed squirrels, turkeys, white-tailed deer, and songbirds.

TRY THIS!

PLANT YOUR OWN TREE

It's not hard to grow your own tree from a seedling. Here's what you need:

- A seedling of a tree that grows well in your area. Some local nurseries, lumberyards, and the Arbor Day Foundation give these away for free. Look for one with bare roots (not in a container).
- A shovel
- Patience! Trees are slow growers.

Then follow these easy steps:

1. Before planting, soak the roots in water for three to six hours.
2. In a sunny spot, not too close to a house or wall, dig a hole that's as deep as the tree roots and a little wider.
3. Place the roots into the hole, no deeper than they are long. Spread the roots out and fill in the hole with dug-up soil.
4. Clear away grass for three feet (1 m) around the tree.
5. Water the tree so the soil is very wet.

WIDE LEAVES WITH FIVE TO NINE DEEP, POINTED LOBES

10s spotters

CAP COVERS ONE-QUARTER OF SHALLOW ACORN.

Post Oak

Quercus stellata HEIGHT 35–60 ft (10.5–18.5 m)
 · SHAPE Small to medium size, short trunk, broad crown
 · LEAVES Alternate, simple, 3–6 in (7.5–15 cm), lobed
 · FLOWERS Catkins · FRUITS Acorns · RANGE Eastern
 and central United States · HABITAT Dry forests,
 mountain slopes, plains · OTHER NAME Iron Oak

The Post Oak takes its common name from one of its common uses: Its strong, long-lasting wood is used to make fence posts. This smallish tree has gnarled branches and scaly brown or gray bark. Its leaves have varied shapes, but they often have two broad, square lobes sticking out from their centers, like a cross.

EXPERT'S CIRCLE

DON'T BE FOOLED

Don't expect to see acorns from young oak trees. It can take 20 years or more for an oak to bear acorns—its first seeds. Often, it doesn't grow a good crop for 50 years or more. In some seasons, an oak might make thousands of acorns. In other seasons, it will produce just a few. For acorns in the red oak group (see page 79 bottom) the ripening season lasts two years, while acorns in the white oak group (see page 78) ripen in a one-year season.

LEAVES WITH FIVE TO SEVEN ROUNDED LOBES, OFTEN WITH WIDE, SQUARE CENTRAL LOBES

CAP COVERS HALF OF ACORN.

90 BEECH (FAGACEAE)

Black Oak

Quercus velutina • HEIGHT 50–80 ft (15–24.5 m) • SHAPE Medium size, tall trunk, oval crown • LEAVES Alternate, simple, 4–10 in (10–25.5 cm), lobed • FLOWERS Catkins • FRUITS Acorns • RANGE Southern Canada, eastern and central United States • HABITAT Dry, sunny slopes • OTHER NAMES Eastern Black Oak, Yellow Oak

The Black Oak is found throughout the eastern half of the United States, from Maine to Oklahoma. It earns its common name because the bark of older trees is dark brown, almost black. Another common name, Yellow Oak, comes from the fact that its inner bark is a yellowish color. And it's part of the red oak group of oak trees, as you can tell by its pointed leaves. No matter what its name, it is a good shade tree whose acorns feed a wide range of wildlife, from deer to blue jays.

SHINY LEAVES WITH FIVE TO NINE POINTED LOBES

....

Live Oak

Quercus virginiana • HEIGHT 50–80 ft (15–24.5 m) • SHAPE Medium to tall; short, wide trunk; very broad crown • LEAVES Alternate, simple, 2–5 in (5–12.5 cm), long oval • FLOWERS Catkins • FRUITS Acorns • RANGE Coastal plain from Virginia to Texas • HABITAT Woods, uplands; yards, roadsides • OTHER NAMES Southern Live Oak, Virginia Live Oak, Coastal Live Oak

STIFF, WAXY, SLENDER OVAL LEAVES, SOMETIMES TOOTHED

Long-lived and fast growing, the Live Oak is a majestic tree. Its trunk is thick, and its branches are very long. Sometimes they grow so wide that they touch the ground and then bend up again. The tree's leafy crown is often broader than the tree is tall. In some places, a hairy, dangling plant called Spanish moss hangs down from its branches, giving the Live Oak a spooky look.

BE A TREE HUGGER!

Live Oak wood is very hard and strong. It was a favorite wood of shipbuilders in the 18th and 19th centuries. The famous sailing ship U.S.S. *Constitution* was built partly of Live Oak wood. In the war of 1812, cannonballs bounced right off the ship's sides, earning it the nickname Old Ironsides.

TREE-MENDOUS: HOW A FOREST GROWS

Disturbance

A fire sweeps through a forest. A logging company cuts down a wide area of trees. The ground is left bare. This is called "disturbance." The natural landscape has been disturbed—changed—by some outside force.

TREES IN THIS GIANT SEQUOIA FOREST IN CALIFORNIA ARE HUNDREDS OF YEARS OLD.

A forest full of tall trees may look as if it has been there forever. But forests grow and change just like people do. You can tell if a forest is young or middle-aged or old by the kinds of trees that grow in it. The process of changing from one set of trees to another is called "succession." One kind of plant succeeds, or follows, another. A forest will grow up, grow old, burn down (or get cut down), and start again. Check out the forests near you and figure out how old they might be by matching them to the following descriptions.

Pioneers

Shrubs and baby trees start to grow in the open areas. The new trees are different from the ones that grew there before. They are trees that grow best in full sunlight. They grow fast. They do well on bare, rocky spots. Aspens, redcedars, and pine trees are common pioneer species.

Young Forest

As the pioneer trees grow tall, they cast shade underneath them. Different kinds of trees, ones that like the shade, start growing under them. They compete with the older trees for food and habitat. The young forest is a mix of trees that like sun and trees that like shade, such as firs and maples.

Climax Forest

The short-lived, sun-loving trees die off. Mixed groups of slow-growing, shade-tolerant trees take over. The forest is dark and has moist, rich soil. If the climax forest isn't disturbed by fires, storms, or logging, it will stay this way for hundreds of years. These very old, undisturbed stands of trees are called "old-growth forests." They are rare and special to visit.

Witch Hazel

Hamamelis virginiana HEIGHT 15–30 ft (4.5–9 m) · SHAPE Small, sometimes shrublike, one or more trunks, irregular crown · LEAVES Alternate, simple, 3–6 in (7.5–15 cm), oval, scalloped edges · FLOWERS Yellow, 4 petals · FRUITS Green to brown capsules · RANGE Eastern Canada, eastern United States · HABITAT Shady woods, swamps · OTHER NAMES Common Witch-hazel, American Witch-hazel

The Witch Hazel is a small tree with odd habits. Unlike most other plants, it blooms in the fall. Its bright yellow, spidery flowers appear even while the tree is dropping its leaves. Around the same time, the capsules that hold its seeds explode. They burst open with a pop and shoot out their seeds up to 30 feet (9 m) away. A liquid made from Witch Hazel bark and leaves is used to soothe the skin around bruises and insect bites.

NAME GAME

The "witch" in the name Witch Hazel probably comes from the old English word "wych," meaning "bend." Early American settlers believed that they could use Witch Hazel twigs to find water underground. Supposedly, the cut pieces of Witch Hazel would bend toward the ground above a water source—but there is no scientific explanation for this!

OVAL LEAVES WITH ROUND OR WEDGE-SHAPED BASE

BRIGHT YELLOW, FOUR-PETALED FALL FLOWERS

Sweetgum

Liquidambar styraciflua HEIGHT 50–150 ft (15–46 m) · SHAPE Medium size to tall, straight trunk, cone-shaped crown · LEAVES Alternate, simple, 4–7 in (10–18 cm), star-shaped · FLOWERS Tiny green clusters · FRUITS Spiky brown balls · RANGE Eastern to southeastern United States to Mississippi and Ohio Valleys · HABITAT Swamps, upland woods, fields · OTHER NAMES Redgum, Sapgum

The tall Sweetgum is a common southeastern tree. It's known for its big, star-shaped leaves, which turn red, yellow, orange, and purple in the autumn. It's also known for its spiky brown fruits, called gumballs, which fall to the ground in winter and can be painful if you step on them. Sweetgums release a juice that can be boiled into a sticky gum. Their wood is often made into shiny furniture, barrels, and boxes. Because it does not splinter easily, the wood is also used in ice pop sticks and chopsticks.

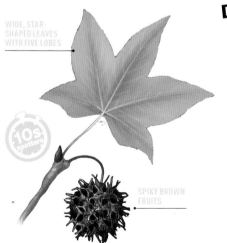

WIDE, STAR-SHAPED LEAVES WITH FIVE LOBES

SPIKY BROWN FRUITS

EXPERT'S CIRCLE

DON'T BE FOOLED People really hate the Sweetgum's spiky gumballs. So tree scientists have made a tree variety that doesn't have any fruits at all. Its scientific name is *Liquidambar styraciflua* 'Rotundiloba.'

Sassafras

Sassafras albidum HEIGHT 30–60 ft (9–18.5 m) · SHAPE Medium size, thick trunk or many trunks, round crown · LEAVES Alternate, simple, 3–7 in (7.5–18 cm), oval, or 2–3 lobes · FLOWERS Small, greenish clusters · FRUITS Blue, berrylike, on red stalks · RANGE Eastern United States · HABITAT Woods, fields, ridges · OTHER NAMES White Sassafras, Ague Tree

The Sassafras tree is easy to pick out. Its leaves often have lobes that make them look like mittens. Sometimes leaves with no lobes, one lobe, or two lobes all grow on the same tree. The leaves are bright yellow and orange in autumn. The tree has a spicy, fruity smell. For centuries, Native Americans and early settlers used Sassafras bark, roots, and leaves as food and medicine. The roots were used to make root beer, cough medicine, and tea, among many other things. The leaves are still ground up to make a spice called filé that gives flavor to a soup called gumbo.

BE A TREE HUGGER!

Crush a Sassafras leaf in your hand and take a sniff. It smells like Froot Loops!

10s spotter

MALE FLOWER HAS NINE STAMENS (FEMALE HAS A CENTRAL PISTIL).

LOBED LEAVES

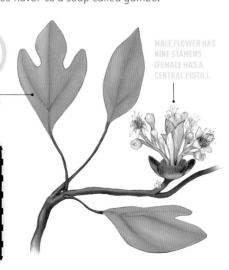

DANGER!

Nowadays, doctors say that you shouldn't eat or drink anything made from Sassafras bark or wood. It has a chemical that might hurt your liver.

California Laurel

Umbellularia californica HEIGHT **23–100 ft (7–30.5 m)** SHAPE **Small to tall; short trunk or many trunks; dense, round crown** LEAVES **Alternate, simple, 2–4 in (5–10 cm), narrow, pointed** FLOWERS **Yellowish clusters** FRUITS **Small, green, fleshy berries** RANGE **Oregon to California** HABITAT **Coastal forests, mountain slopes, canyons** OTHER NAMES **Oregon Myrtle, California Bay, Pepperwood**

The California Laurel can be small and shrubby or tall and densely covered with leaves, depending upon where it grows. It is best known for its leaves, which have an oil with a strong, peppery smell. People used to make headbands out of the leaves, believing they would ease the pain of headaches. Other people claimed that the oil actually *gave* them headaches. No wonder the California Laurel is sometimes called the "Headache Tree." Don't eat laurel leaves, whether you have a headache or not. They can make you sick.

NARROW, POINTED LEAVES

Tuliptree

Liriodendron tulipifera HEIGHT **80–120 ft (24.5–36.5 m)** SHAPE **Tall, straight trunk, pyramid-shaped crown** LEAVES **Alternate, simple, 3–7 in (7.5–18 cm), wide, lobed** FLOWERS **Bright yellow or green, cup-shaped** FRUITS **Narrow cones of samaras** RANGE **Eastern United States** HABITAT **Damp forests, parks** OTHER NAMES **Tulip Poplar, Yellow Poplar**

WIDE, FOUR-LOBED LEAVES

The fast-growing Tuliptree is the tallest broadleaf tree in the East. Tuliptrees are often called Tulip Poplars, but they're not poplar trees. They are actually a kind of magnolia. The shape of their four-lobed leaves looks a bit like a tulip, and their flowers also look a little like tulip flowers. The flowers grow in the top of the tall tree's crown, but you can see them when they drop to the ground. Tuliptree fruits are winged samaras, like maple seeds. They cling together in upright cones at first, and then they gradually pull apart and fly away one by one.

DANGER!

Don't stand near a Tulip Poplar during a storm. It is one of the trees most frequently struck by lightning in forests and yards because it is usually the tallest tree around.

LONG, POINTED, OVAL LEAVES

Cucumber-tree

Magnolia acuminata HEIGHT 60–80 ft (18.5–24.5 m) · SHAPE Medium size, straight trunk, cone-shaped crown · LEAVES Alternate, simple, 6–10 in (15–25.5 cm), oval, pointed · FLOWERS Yellow, bell-shaped · FRUITS Green to red conelike cluster · RANGE Louisiana to New York; Ontario · HABITAT Damp forests, slopes · OTHER NAMES Cucumber Magnolia, Yellow Cucumber-tree

The Cucumber-tree is named for its little cone-shaped fruits, which—when they are young and green—look like cucumbers. It's a species of magnolia, and like other magnolias it has lovely flowers, ranging from greenish yellow to bright yellow. The Cucumber-tree is spread widely through the East. It does well in colder temperatures and is the only magnolia tree found in Canada.

THICK, SHINY, POINTED, OVAL LEAVES

Southern Magnolia

Magnolia grandiflora HEIGHT 65–95 ft (20–29 m) · SHAPE Medium size; tall, straight trunk; rounded crown · LEAVES Alternate, simple, 5–8 in (12.5–20.5 cm), oval, pointed · FLOWERS Large, white, cup-shaped · FRUITS Green to red conelike cluster · RANGE Coast of North Carolina to Texas · HABITAT Damp forests; yards, parks · OTHER NAMES Evergreen Magnolia, Bull-Bay

The Southern Magnolia is the queen of magnolia trees. Its big, beautiful, sweet-smelling flowers make it a popular choice for yards and parks. Its evergreen leaves are also handsome. Thick and leathery, they are shiny green above and rusty green underneath. Though this magnolia is native to the South, it is planted as far north as New York State. In fact, Southern Magnolias are planted around the world.

LARGE, CREAMY WHITE, SWEET-SMELLING FLOWERS

EXPERT'S CIRCLE

DON'T BE FOOLED Magnolias are an ancient genus of trees. The first ones appeared about 95 million years ago. Like some other ancient flowering plants, its flowers don't have petals. Instead, they have petal-like parts called tepals.

Sweetbay

Magnolia virginiana HEIGHT 20–60 ft (6–18.5 m)
SHAPE Small to medium size, sometimes shrublike, one or many trunks, narrow crown • LEAVES Alternate, simple, 4–6 in (10–15 cm), oval, pointed • FLOWERS White, cup-shaped • FRUITS Green to red oval cluster • RANGE Coastal plain, New Jersey to Texas • HABITAT Stream banks, swamps, damp woods • OTHER NAMES Swamp Magnolia, Sweetbay Magnolia, Laurel Magnolia

In the North, the Sweetbay is shrubby and drops most of its leaves in the fall. In the South, it is a medium-size tree that holds on to most of its leaves all winter. The Sweetbay's leaves are shiny green on top and silvery gray underneath. When the wind blows the leaves around, the tree seems to ripple with light. Like other magnolias, it has beautiful, sweet-smelling flowers. Sweetbay flowers are white with a lemony scent, while other kinds of Magnolia flowers can be yellow, pink, or green, with a range of good smells.

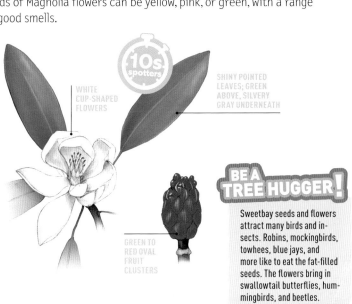

WHITE CUP-SHAPED FLOWERS

SHINY POINTED LEAVES; GREEN ABOVE, SILVERY GRAY UNDERNEATH

GREEN TO RED OVAL FRUIT CLUSTERS

BE A TREE HUGGER!

Sweetbay seeds and flowers attract many birds and insects. Robins, mockingbirds, towhees, blue jays, and more like to eat the fat-filled seeds. The flowers bring in swallowtail butterflies, hummingbirds, and beetles.

Osage Orange

Maclura pomifera HEIGHT 40–60 ft (12–18.5 m) · SHAPE Medium size; short trunk; wide, dense crown · LEAVES Alternate, simple, 3–5 in (7.5–12.5 cm), oval, pointed · FLOWERS Hanging or round clusters · FRUITS Large, round, bumpy, green · RANGE Native to south-central United States but planted throughout eastern United States · HABITAT Forests, abandoned fields · OTHER NAMES Hedge Apple, Horse Apple, Bois-d'Arc

The Osage Orange is not an orange tree—in fact, it's related to fig trees. It gets its name from two things. Its bark and wood have an orange tint, and the fruits produced by the female trees are clustered into large, bumpy balls that look like oranges. The balls are green, though, and taste bad. Sharp thorns grow from the stiff, tangled branches. Ranchers used to plant the trees close together as a kind of prickly fence. Such a hedge was "horse high, bull strong, and pig tight," according to the *Prairie Farmer* newspaper. The wood doesn't rot easily and is sometimes used to build fence posts. Some posts have lasted more than 100 years. The Osage Orange is a pioneer tree, meaning that it is one of the first to grow in open pastures and fields.

NAME GAME

Some other common names of the Osage Orange—Hedge Apple and Horse Apple—refer to the tree's round fruit. They're not apples any more than they are oranges, though. They're clusters of little fruits. The common name Bois d'Arc means "wood of the bow" in French. French settlers named the tree after seeing Osage Indians making bows from its wood.

OVAL, POINTED LEAVES

SHARP THORNS

LARGE, ROUND, GREEN FRUIT CLUSTERS

DANGER!

Don't touch the Osage Orange. Its branches are covered with nasty thorns. Ouch!

White Mulberry

ROUNDED OVAL LEAVES, POINTED TIPS, SOMETIMES LOBED, SMOOTH ON TOP

Morus alba HEIGHT 30–50 ft (9–15 m) · SHAPE Small, short trunk; wide, rounded crown · LEAVES Alternate, simple, 2–7 in (5–18 cm), rounded, pointed oval, sometimes lobed · FLOWERS Small catkins · FRUITS White, pink, or purple, berrylike · RANGE Native to China, widespread in United States · HABITAT Edges of woods and fields; streets · OTHER NAMES Silkworm Mulberry, Chinese White Mulberry, Russian Mulberry

The White Mulberry is native to China, where for thousands of years it has fed the silkworms that make Chinese silk. People brought the tree to the United States in 1607, hoping to start up a silk business there. Silkworms didn't like American weather, but the trees did. They spread widely across the continent. Now, the trees are considered an invasive plant: one that causes harm to native plants and crowds them out. White Mulberries have berrylike fruits. Birds like the sweet berries, but they can be a squishy mess once they've fallen to the ground.

BE A TREE HUGGER!

When the catkins of the White Mulberry have matured in the spring, pollen—a yellow dust found in flowers—bursts out from the tree's flowers at about 350 miles an hour (563 km/h). That's more than half the speed of sound! It is the fastest known movement made by any plant.

Red Mulberry

ROUNDED OVAL LEAVES, POINTED TIP, SOMETIMES LOBED, ROUGH ON TOP

Morus rubra HEIGHT 20–60 ft (6–18.5 m) · SHAPE Small to medium size; short trunk; wide, thick crown · LEAVES Alternate, simple, 4–5 in (10–12.5 cm), rounded, pointed oval, sometimes lobed · FLOWERS Small catkins · FRUITS Red to dark purple, berrylike · RANGE Eastern United States, southern Ontario · HABITAT Woods, pastures, river valleys; roadsides · OTHER NAMES None

Unlike its relative the White Mulberry, the Red Mulberry is native to the United States. It is known for its sweet purple fruits, a favorite of birds. People often bake the fruit into jams and jellies, but the berries don't keep very well on their own. They also make a mess on the ground when they drop off the trees in summer.

EXPERT'S CIRCLE

DON'T BE FOOLED It can be hard to tell Red and White Mulberries (above) apart. Try touching their leaves. Red Mulberry leaves are usually rough on top. White Mulberry leaves are usually smooth.

Tasmanian Bluegum

Eucalyptus globulus HEIGHT 100–180 ft (30.5–55 m) · SHAPE Very tall, straight trunk, narrow crown · LEAVES Alternate, simple, 4–11 in (10–28 cm), narrow, pointed · FLOWERS Round, white, fluffy · FRUITS Woody capsule · RANGE Native to Australia; West Coast, Hawaii · HABITAT Coastal areas, fields; streets · OTHER NAME Bluegum Eucalyptus

The Tasmanian Bluegum, a kind of eucalyptus tree, was brought to the United States from Australia in the 19th century. The tall trees then spread up and down the Pacific coast, and today they are invasive in California. You can spot them by their tall, slender shape, hanging narrow leaves, and peeling bark. The minty-smelling oil in their leaves and twigs is used in medicine and toothpaste. Because of their bark and oils, the trees catch fire easily, and they blaze like a torch during wildfires.

BE A TREE HUGGER!

The tallest Tasmanian Bluegum in the United States stands 218 feet (66.45 m) tall in Stern Grove Park, San Francisco, California.

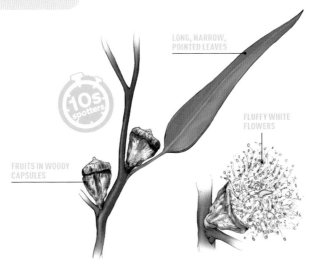

LONG, NARROW, POINTED LEAVES

FLUFFY WHITE FLOWERS

FRUITS IN WOODY CAPSULES

Water Tupelo

OVAL, POINTED LEAVES WITH A FEW TEETH

Nyssa aquatica HEIGHT 50–80 ft (15–24.5 m) · SHAPE Medium size to tall; tall, straight trunk; wide, round crown · LEAVES Alternate, simple, 4–8 in (10–20.5 cm), long oval, pointed, a few teeth · FLOWERS Small greenish clusters · FRUITS Blue or purple, berrylike · RANGE Southeast coast, Virginia to Texas, Mississippi River Valley · HABITAT Flooded areas, swamps · OTHER NAMES Cottongum, Swamp Tupelo

Water Tupelos like to get their feet wet. They grow best in warm swamps and other flooded places, often springing up right out of the water. In these areas, their trunks widen out to a broad base, like a giant elephant's foot. The Water Tupelo's slender, berrylike fruits drop into the water and float until they find a place to take root. The tree's flowers are small, but they are popular with bees, which make tasty Tupelo honey.

NAME GAME

The Water Tupelo's genus name, *Nyssa,* refers to a mountain in Greek mythology that was the home of water nymphs.

Blackgum

Nyssa sylvatica HEIGHT 60–80 ft (18.5–24.5 m) · SHAPE Medium size; tall, straight trunk; cone-shaped crown · LEAVES Alternate, simple, 2–6 in (5–15 cm), oval · FLOWERS Small greenish clusters · FRUITS Purple or black, berrylike · RANGE Eastern United States, southern Ontario · HABITAT Damp forests, swamp edges, slopes · OTHER NAMES Black Tupelo, Sourgum, Pepperidge

OVAL LEAVES, SHINY GREEN ON TOP; REDDISH IN AUTUMN

Tall and straight, the Blackgum has bright red, gold, and purple leaves in the autumn. Like its relative the Water Tupelo, it likes wet areas, but it can also grow on dry hillsides and mountain slopes. The tree often has hollow spaces in its trunk. Birds and mammals nest in these spaces, and bees build their hives there. In older trees, the brownish bark is thick and scaly, like alligator skin.

American Sycamore

Platanus occidentalis HEIGHT **60–100 ft (18.5–30.5 m)** · SHAPE **Tall, thick trunk, wide crown** · LEAVES **Alternate, simple, 4–8 in (10–20.5 cm), lobed** · FLOWERS **Small greenish or reddish clusters** · FRUITS **Small round clusters** · RANGE **Eastern United States** · HABITAT **Stream banks, rivers, swamps, abandoned fields, streets** · OTHER NAMES **American Plane Tree, Buttonball Tree**

The fast-growing American Sycamore is a big, impressive tree. The largest stand more than 120 feet (36.5 m) tall and measure 13 feet (4 m) around the trunk. The tree's flaky bark peels off in patches. Underneath, white, yellow, and brown inner bark shows through. The American Sycamore grows well in wet spots, but it also is one of the first trees to spring up in abandoned fields. It is often planted along streets because traffic pollution doesn't hurt it.

NAME GAME

English settlers named the American Sycamore after the European Sycamore Maple. The two trees have similar leaves, but the American Sycamore is actually in the plane tree family.

THE FRUIT, CALLED AN ACHENE, IS A FUZZY GREEN BALL ON A LONG STEM.

WIDE LEAVES, THREE TO FIVE SHARP LOBES

PARACHUTE-LIKE HAIRS ON SEEDS FOR SCATTERING

London Plane Tree

Platanus × acerifolia HEIGHT 75–100 ft (23–30.5 m) · SHAPE Tall,
thick trunk, wide crown · LEAVES Alternate, simple, 4–8 in (10–20.5 cm),
lobed · FLOWERS Small greenish or reddish clusters · FRUITS Small
round clusters, 2 to a stalk · RANGE Widespread, particularly in the East
· HABITAT City plantings in streets and parks · OTHER NAMES None

The big, handsome London Plane Tree looks
a lot like the American Sycamore. There's a
good reason for that. It is a hybrid—a mix of two
different plants. The London Plane Tree is a cross
between the American Sycamore and the Oriental
Plane Tree. The London Plane Tree's smooth bark is not as colorful as
the American Sycamore's, and the tree's ball-like cluster of seeds grow
two to a stalk. Because the London Plane Tree grows well in polluted
air, it is planted in many cities in the United States and England.

WIDE LEAVES WITH THREE
TO SEVEN POINTED LOBES

California Sycamore

Platanus racemosa HEIGHT 40–100 ft (12–30.5 m) · SHAPE Medium size
to tall, trunk sometimes leaning or divided, wide crown · LEAVES Alternate,
simple, 5–10 in (12.5–25.5 cm), lobed · FLOWERS Small reddish green clusters
· FRUITS Small round clusters, 3–7 to a stalk · RANGE California · HABITAT
Valleys, foothills, waterways · OTHER NAME Western Sycamore

Like other plane trees, the California
Sycamore is a stout, broad-crowned tree. Its
bark peels into patches in young trees, but in
older trees the bark is dark and ridged. The big
leathery leaves have deeper lobes than those of
other plane trees. Three to seven round fruits
dangle on a long stalk like beads on a necklace.

WIDE LEAVES
WITH THREE TO
FIVE DEEP LOBES

Laugh Out Loud! Why did the plane tree miss so much school?

Because it was a sycamore!

Saskatoon

Amelanchier alnifolia HEIGHT 30–40 ft (9–12 m) · SHAPE Small, sometimes shrublike, slender trunk or many trunks · LEAVES Alternate, simple, 1–2 in (2.5–5 cm), oval, toothed at tip · FLOWERS White, 5 petals · FRUITS Small, berrylike, blue-purple, in clusters · RANGE Canada, western, central, and eastern United States · HABITAT Forests, slopes, stream banks · OTHER NAMES Serviceberry, Pacific Serviceberry, Western Serviceberry, Juneberry

The small, slender Saskatoon lights up with white flowers in spring. However, it's best known for its fruits. The bluish purple berries look a lot like blueberries, and like blueberries they are sweet and tasty when they're ripe. People cook them into pies, jams, and syrups. Animals also enjoy the trees. Deer, moose, and rabbits eat the leaves and twigs. Bears and many birds, including blue jays, mockingbirds, robins, and crows, eat the berries.

NAME GAME

The Canadian city of Saskatoon is named after this berry. The name comes from a phrase used by the Cree people meaning "early berry."

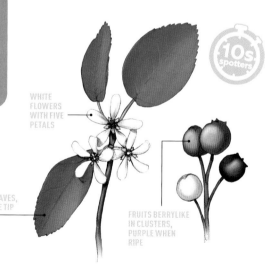

WHITE FLOWERS WITH FIVE PETALS

SMALL OVAL LEAVES, TOOTHED AT THE TIP

FRUITS BERRYLIKE IN CLUSTERS, PURPLE WHEN RIPE

Hawthorn

Crataegus spp. **HEIGHT** 15–50 ft (4.5–15 m)
- **SHAPE** Small, sometimes shrublike, short trunk or many trunks, round crown • **LEAVES** Alternate, simple, 0.75–4 in (2–10 cm), toothed, usually oval, sometimes lobed • **FLOWERS** White, pink, or red, 5 petals
- **FRUITS** Round, red, berrylike • **RANGE** United States and Canada • **HABITAT** Meadows, woods, riverbanks • **OTHER NAME** Thorn-apple

There are so many species of Hawthorns, and they are so hard to tell apart, that even tree scientists get confused. In this entry, we'll just describe Hawthorns in general. These short, shrubby trees bear open white flowers in spring. On some trees the flowers smell sweet, but on most they are stinky. The red, berrylike fruit, known as a haw, looks like a tiny apple. The other half of the tree's name, "thorn," comes from the long, sharp thorns that stick out of its branchlets. Songbirds like to nest in the Hawthorn's thorny branches and eat their haws.

RED, BERRYLIKE FRUIT

SMALL, TOOTHED LEAVES

DANGER!

Don't grab Hawthorn branches. Their thorns can be up to four inches (10 cm) long—and they're sharp. Yikes!

WHITE FLOWERS WITH FIVE PETALS

EXPERT'S CIRCLE

DON'T BE FOOLED When a scientific name lists the genus and then "spp.," as above, that means there are many species within that genus.

WHITE FLOWERS
WITH FIVE PETALS

American Plum

Prunus americana HEIGHT 15–30 ft (4.5–9 m) · SHAPE Small, sometimes shrublike, short trunk or many trunks, broad crown · LEAVES Alternate, simple, 2–4 in (5–10 cm), oval, toothed · FLOWERS White, 5 petals · FRUITS Round, fleshy, orange to red · RANGE Eastern and central United States · HABITAT Woods, stream banks, fields · OTHER NAME Wild Plum

The American Plum grows in the wild across much of the United States. Short and broad, it blooms with lovely but nasty-smelling white flowers in spring. Its fruits, appearing in summer, are red and fleshy plums, about one inch (2.5 cm) across. People can eat them, although they are not very sweet. With some added sugar, the plums are often cooked into pies and jams. Birds like to nest in the tree's thick crown, and deer nibble on the leaves and branches.

Mexican Plum

Prunus mexicana HEIGHT 15–30 ft (4.5–9 m) · SHAPE Small, sometimes shrublike, short trunk, broad crown · LEAVES Alternate, simple, 2–4 in (5–10 cm), oval, toothed · FLOWERS White, 5 petals · FRUITS Round, fleshy, red to purple · RANGE Midwest, south-central United States · HABITAT Woods, hillsides · OTHER NAMES None

OVAL, TOOTHED
LEAVES

The Mexican Plum tree is similar to the American Plum. However, it has smaller fruit and usually only a single trunk. It also lacks the sharp, thorny twigs that grow on the American Plum. Mexican Plums are lovely in the spring, when they are covered with white flowers. Their plums are slightly sour but can be made into jams and jellies.

EXPERT'S CIRCLE

DON'T BE FOOLED Plum trees belong to the rose family—the same kind of plants that might grow as beautiful flowering bushes in your yard. Cherry trees, apple trees, pears, peaches, hawthorns, and serviceberries also belong to this family. All of these trees have five-petaled flowers. Many have fleshy, sweet fruit.

Black Cherry

Prunus serotina HEIGHT **30–110 ft (9–33.5 m)**
· SHAPE **Small to tall; straight, thick trunk; crown narrow to broad** · LEAVES **Alternate, simple, 2–6 in (5–15 cm), slender pointed oval, toothed** · FLOWERS **White, 5 petals, in hanging clusters** · FRUITS **Round, small, red to purplish black, in hanging clusters** · RANGE **East to Midwest; Southwest** · HABITAT **Woods and forests, fields and fencerows** · OTHER NAMES **Wild Cherry, Rum Cherry, Mountain Black Cherry**

Tall and fast growing, the Black Cherry is found in woods and fields across much of the United States. It is valued for its gorgeous, hard, red-brown wood. The tree's small cherries have a strong, sharp taste. With sugar, they are often made into juices and jams. Black Cherry trees spread easily, their seeds carried from place to place by birds. People brought the trees to Europe in the 1600s. This turned out to be a bad idea, because the trees are now spreading too fast.

SMALL CHERRIES, ORANGE TO BLACK

DANGER!

Black Cherry leaves, bark, and seeds have some poisonous chemicals. Deer can eat them without being harmed—but don't try eating them yourself! Only the fruit is safe to eat for humans.

NARROW, POINTED, TOOTHED LEAVES

FLOWERS IN HANGING WHITE CLUSTERS

Klamath Plum

Prunus subcordata HEIGHT **To 25 ft (7.5 m)** • SHAPE **Small, sometimes shrublike, thick crown** • LEAVES **Alternate, simple, 1–3 in (2.5–7.5 cm), rounded oval, toothed** • FLOWERS **White or pink, 5 petals, in clusters** • FRUITS **Small, red or yellow, berrylike** • RANGE **California and Oregon** • HABITAT **Woods, dry mountains slopes and valleys** • OTHER NAMES **Oregon Plum, Pacific Plum**

ROUNDED, OVAL, POINTED LEAVES WITH TOOTHED EDGES

PINK OR WHITE FLOWERS

The Klamath Plum is the only plum tree found near the Pacific coast. Small and thorny, the trees sometimes grow together in tangled rows. Their little fruits are tart in taste, but people sometimes cook them or eat them dried. Early European settlers in the West liked the fruit and planted the trees around their settlements.

Callery Pear

Pyrus calleryana HEIGHT **30–50 ft (9–15 m)** • SHAPE **Small to medium size, single trunk, cone-shaped crown** • LEAVES **Alternate, simple, 2–3 in (5–7.5 cm), pointed oval** • FLOWERS **White, 5 petals, in clusters** • FRUITS **Small, round, berrylike, in clusters** • RANGE **Native to Asia; eastern United States to Texas** • HABITAT **Streets, yards, parks** • OTHER NAMES **None**

WHITE FIVE-PETALED FLOWERS IN CLUSTERS

In the 19th century, American pear trees were suffering from a disease called fire blight. So travelers to China brought back seeds from Asian pear trees, hoping to breed a new kind of pear that would resist the disease. This new tree, the Callery Pear, did resist fire blight. It was a healthy tree that spread quickly through the East. People planted it in yards to enjoy its lovely white flowers and attractive shape. Now, though, it is spreading too much and crowding out other plants. Tree scientists tell us not to plant any more Callery Pears—they grow too well even without our help!

The Callery Pear is an invasive species. It is introduced to a new habitat from another habitat and harms native plants. Plants brought in from other countries may have no natural enemies in their new location, so they can grow far and wide, invading the area and leaving little room for the natural plants.

Sweet Crabapple

Malus coronaria HEIGHT **10–30 ft (3–9 m)**
· SHAPE **Small, short trunk, broad crown** · LEAVES
**Alternate, simple, 3–4 in (7.5–10 cm), oval,
sometimes lobed** · FLOWERS **Pink or white,
5 petals, in clusters** · FRUITS **Small green
apples** · RANGE **New York, Pennsylvania to
Great Lakes** · HABITAT **Forest edges, fences,
valleys** · OTHER NAME **Garland Crab**

This small, sometimes shrubby tree is one of four species of apple trees that are native to North America. Sweet Crabapple fruits aren't good to eat. They're small, green, and sour. But Sweet Crabapple trees are sweetly pretty when they're covered with pink flowers in the spring. That's why some people plant them in their yards.

BROAD,
OVAL LEAVES,
SOMETIMES LOBED

PINK FIVE-PETALED
FLOWERS

SMALL, ONE-INCH (2.5-CM),
ROUND GREEN FRUITS

BE A TREE HUGGER!

Crabapples are closely related to common orchard apple trees—the kind that grow big fruit you might buy from the store. The main difference between crabapple trees and orchard apple trees is the size of their fruit. Orchard apples are more than two inches (5 cm) wide. Crabapples are smaller than two inches wide.

TREE-MENDOUS: MAGICAL TREES

Oak

Many different cultures have different traditions involving the tall, long-lived oak tree. In ancient Britain, Druids (Celtic wise men) met in oak groves to practice their magic. Kings wore crowns of oak leaves to show that they were blessed by the gods. In ancient Greece, the sacred oaks of Dodona could "speak" to priestesses through the rustling of their leaves.

A CARPET OF BLUEBELLS COVERS THE FLOOR OF A DECIDUOUS FOREST LIT BY EARLY MORNING SUN.

People are grateful to trees for their shade, shelter, fruit, and wood. They respect them for their great size and age. Because of these characteristics, trees play an important part in myths and legends from around the world. In many stories, they connect humans to the spirit world. Here are a few beliefs about these leafy giants.

Banyan

Wide and winding, banyan trees grow in Asia and Hawaii. People in many countries believe they are holy or have magical powers. In Hong Kong, people write wishes on pieces of paper and hang them up under two special banyans, called the Lam Tsuen wishing trees. Supposedly, these wishes will then come true.

Ash

In Norse mythology, the world tree, Yggdrasil, is an ash. This immense tree holds the worlds of men, giants, and dwarves in its branches and roots. At its base is a well, the home of three wise women who spend their days carving everyone's fortune into the tree's bark. A dragon gnaws on the tree's roots, and a squirrel, Ratatosk, carries messages up and down the trunk.

Western Redcedar

Native Americans of the Northwest have a lot of respect for the towering Western Redcedar tree, known as the "tree of life." Some people carry little pieces of the tree inside pouches to protect them against sickness. They may sweep fresh-smelling Western Redcedar branches through the air to clean and bless a new house.

Pussy Willow

Salix discolor HEIGHT 20–30 ft (6–9 m) · SHAPE Small, sometimes shrublike, one trunk or many trunks, irregular crown · LEAVES Alternate, simple, 2–5 in (5–12.5 cm), slender pointed oval · FLOWERS Catkins · FRUITS Capsules · RANGE Canada, northeastern United States to Smoky Mountains · HABITAT Wet areas, stream banks, ponds · OTHER NAMES None

Like other willows, the Pussy Willow grows best in wet places. The little trees come in male and female types. In spring, the male trees grow soft, gray catkins that look like cat paws. Catkins on female trees are greenish and not so soft. In the summer, the Pussy Willow's seed capsules break open and little fluffy seeds float out.

LONG, OVAL LEAVES; GREEN ON TOP AND WHITISH UNDERNEATH

10s spotters

FEMALE CATKINS, GREENISH

MALE CATKINS, SOFT AND GRAY

EXPERT'S CIRCLE

DON'T BE FOOLED Some trees, such as Pussy Willows, come in two separate male and female forms (above). Other trees have male and female flowers on different parts of the same tree. And some trees mix male and female in the same flower.

Bebb Willow

Salix bebbiana HEIGHT 15–25 ft (4.5–7.5 m)
· SHAPE Small, sometimes shrublike, one short trunk or many trunks, round crown · LEAVES Alternate, simple, 1–3 in (2.5–7.5 cm), slender pointed oval · FLOWERS Catkins · FRUITS Capsules · RANGE Canada, northern United States · HABITAT Cool, wet areas, mountains · OTHER NAMES Diamond Willow, Beak Willow

Fast-growing Bebb Willows often spring up in tangled groups. They are known as Diamond Willows because of the diamond-shaped holes in their trunks. These holes are caused by a fungus that grows into the tree. When Bebb Willows are carved, a diamond pattern appears in the cream and red wood. Many animals feed on these willows, including deer, moose, hares, and beavers.

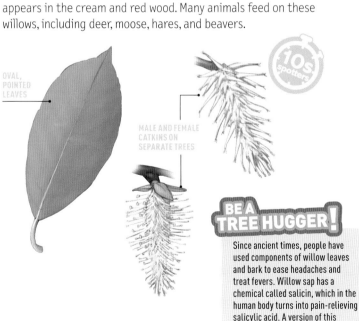

OVAL, POINTED LEAVES

MALE AND FEMALE CATKINS ON SEPARATE TREES

BE A TREE HUGGER!

Since ancient times, people have used components of willow leaves and bark to ease headaches and treat fevers. Willow sap has a chemical called salicin, which in the human body turns into pain-relieving salicylic acid. A version of this chemical is used in aspirin.

Black Willow

Salix nigra HEIGHT 30–60 ft (9–18.5 m) · SHAPE Small to medium size, thick trunk, broad crown · LEAVES Alternate, simple, 3–6 in (7.5–15 cm), narrow, pointed · FLOWERS Catkins · FRUITS Capsules · RANGE Maine to Minnesota, south to Texas · HABITAT Wet areas; streams, lakes, swamps · OTHER NAMES Swamp Willow, American Willow

Unlike most willows, the Black Willow is fairly tall and stout. It grows in swampy places and along streams throughout the eastern and central United States. It gains its name from its rough bark, which is dark brown or black. Black Willow wood is lightweight and used for building toys and wooden boxes. Because the trees grow fast and have dense roots, they are good for planting along stream banks to hold the soil in place.

BE A TREE HUGGER!

People used to make wooden legs out of light, nonsplintery Black Willow wood.

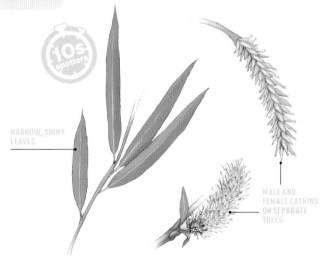

NARROW, SHINY LEAVES

MALE AND FEMALE CATKINS ON SEPARATE TREES

Weeping Willow

Salix babylonica HEIGHT **30–60 ft (9–18.5 m)** · SHAPE **Medium size, thick trunk, round crown with drooping branches** · LEAVES **Alternate, simple, 2–6 in (5–15 cm), narrow, pointed** · FLOWERS **Catkins** · FRUITS **Capsules** · RANGE **Native to China, widespread in United States** · HABITAT **Wet areas, lakes, ponds** · OTHER NAME **Babylon Weeping Willow**

When people talk about willow trees, the Weeping Willow is usually the one they mean. This fast-growing, water-loving tree is famous for its drooping branches, which can touch the ground. In autumn, its skinny leaves turn a bright golden yellow. Weeping Willows were brought to North America from China. People plant them in yards and along waterways because of their beautiful shape. However, the tree's roots tend to grow toward water. This means the roots can grow into water sewers and drains and damage them.

NARROW, POINTED LEAVES

MALE AND FEMALE CATKINS ON SEPARATE TREES

10s spotters

NAME GAME

A famous plant scientist during the 1700s, Carl Linnaeus, named this species *babylonica* because he thought it was a tree mentioned in the Bible. In the Bible verse, people wept and hung their harps on willows beside the rivers of Babylon. However, those trees in ancient Babylon were probably poplars.

Black Cottonwood

Populus trichocarpa HEIGHT **100–165 ft (30.5–50.5 m)**
· SHAPE **Tall; straight, thick trunk; high, open crown** · LEAVES
Alternate, simple, 3–6 in (7.5–15 cm), pointed oval
· FLOWERS **Catkins** · FRUITS **Capsules** · RANGE **Alaska
to U.S. Northwest, Canada** · HABITAT **Stream banks,
riverbanks, wet woods** · OTHER NAMES **Common Black
Cottonwood, Balsam Cottonwood**

The Black Cottonwood is the
tallest natural broadleaf tree
in the West. It's a fast-growing
tree that likes the moist, rich
soil along rivers and streams. Its
pale, lightweight wood is often used
to make furniture and boxes. As with
other cottonwoods, the Black Cottonwood
has white, fluffy seeds that look like tiny pieces
of cotton. After the seeds break free of their
capsules, they float through the air. It looks like
it's snowing in spring!

BE A TREE HUGGER!

Spread by their floating
seeds, Black Cottonwoods
are often pioneer trees—
the first ones to grow in
open spaces.

DROOPING
REDDISH
CATKINS

THICK, POINTED,
OVAL LEAVES

Eastern Cottonwood

Populus deltoides ssp. *deltoides* HEIGHT 80–100 ft (24.5–30.5 m)
· SHAPE Tall, thick trunk, broad crown · LEAVES Alternate, simple, 3–5 in (7.5–12.5 cm), triangular · FLOWERS Catkins · FRUITS Capsules in long, hanging clusters · RANGE Eastern to central United States · HABITAT Stream banks; wet, low forests · OTHER NAMES Carolina Poplar, Southern Cottonwood

The Eastern Cottonwood's tall trunk branches out at the top to hold up a wide, V-shaped crown. Like other cottonwoods, the tree prefers wet sites. In spring, its fluffy seeds float far and wide. At times, the Eastern Cottonwood is a noisy tree. Its leaves hang on long, bendy stems. When the wind blows, they flutter and make rattling sounds.

TRIANGULAR LEAF WITH TOOTHED EDGES, ON LONG STEM

Laugh Out Loud!

Why was the farmer's shirt so scratchy?

It was made from cottonwood!

....

Plains Cottonwood

Populus deltoides ssp. *monilifera* HEIGHT 40–90 ft (12–27.5 m) · SHAPE Tall; thick, branching trunk; broad crown · LEAVES Alternate, simple, 2–3 in (5–7.5 cm), triangular · FLOWERS Catkins · FRUITS Capsules in long, hanging clusters · RANGE Great Plains (Canada to Texas) · HABITAT Rivers, woods, roadsides · OTHER NAMES None

WIDE, TRIANGULAR LEAF WITH ROUNDED TEETH

The Plains Cottonwood is a close relative of the Eastern Cottonwood, but it lives mainly in the center of the country. Its leaves are a little smaller and wider than those of the Eastern Cottonwood, with bigger teeth around the edges. As with other cottonwoods, its catkins appear before its leaves grow in the spring. The cottony seeds then fly away freely on the wind.

EXPERT'S CIRCLE

DON'T BE FOOLED Sometimes a scientific name will list the genus, the species, and also a subspecies. A subspecies is one variety within a species. For instance, the Plains Cottonwood is a subspecies of Eastern Cottonwood (above). In the scientific name, the subspecies name comes after the abbreviation "ssp.," (which stands for "subspecies").

Quaking Aspen

Populus tremuloides HEIGHT 40–60 ft (12–18.5 m) · SHAPE **Medium size; slender, straight trunk; high, rounded crown** · LEAVES **Alternate, simple, 1–3 in (2.5–7.5 cm), rounded oval** · FLOWERS **Catkins** · FRUITS **Capsules in long, hanging clusters** · RANGE **Alaska to Virginia** · HABITAT **Forests, mountains** · OTHER NAMES **American Aspen, Trembling Aspen, Golden Aspen**

With their tall, white trunks and leafy crowns that turn golden in the autumn, Quaking Aspens can look like yellow pom-poms. They shake like pom-poms, too. Their leaves hang on long, bendable stalks and flutter in the lightest winds. Quaking Aspens are the most widespread trees in North America. You can find them from Alaska throughout the western United States and into the Northeast. The only region they don't like is the hot, humid Southeast.

BE A TREE HUGGER!

A Quaking Aspen's roots grow out sideways, sometimes for more than 100 feet (30.5 m). New trees will sprout from these roots. The new trees look like separate plants, but they are part of the original tree. So what looks like a small forest of Quaking Aspens may really be one single tree. In Utah's Bryce Canyon National Park, a Quaking Aspen called Pando, or Trembling Giant, appears to have more than 40,000 separate trunks.

TRIANGULAR OR ROUNDED OVAL, POINTED LEAVES

MALE AND FEMALE CATKINS ON SEPARATE TREES; FEMALE (RIGHT) HOLDS TUFTED SEED CAPSULE

American Basswood

Tilia americana HEIGHT **60–80 ft (18.5–24.5 m)** SHAPE **Medium size, straight to branching trunk, broad crown** LEAVES **Alternate, simple, 5–8 in (12.5–20.5 cm), heart-shaped, pointed** FLOWERS **Small, yellow-white, hanging from leafy bract** FRUITS **Small nutlike balls** RANGE **Eastern and central United States** HABITAT **Damp forests** OTHER NAMES **American Linden, Basswood**

The broad, thickly leaved American Basswood is a friend to wildlife. It often has holes in its big trunk that make ideal nesting places for birds such as woodpeckers and wood ducks. The tree's little nutlike fruits are a favorite food of many small birds and mammals. And its flowers make a nectar that feeds honeybees. People like its soft wood, which can be carved into toys or musical instruments.

HEART-SHAPED, POINTED LEAVES

....

Common Hackberry

Celtis occidentalis HEIGHT **40–60 ft (12–18.5 m)** SHAPE **Medium size, straight trunk, broad crown** LEAVES **Alternate, simple, 2–5 in (5–12.5 cm), pointed oval** FLOWERS **Small, greenish** FRUITS **Orange to purple, berrylike** RANGE **Eastern and central United States** HABITAT **Woods, river valleys, stream banks** OTHER NAMES **Northern Hackberry, American Hackberry**

The Common Hackberry is a widespread tree that can live in many different habitats. It will grow in dry, sandy places, but it prefers the wet ground of river valleys or stream banks. Because it has a dense, broad crown, it makes a good shade tree. In autumn, its berrylike fruits turn purple and sweet and attract hungry birds. Butterflies come to the Common Hackberry to lay their eggs.

SHINY, OVAL, POINTED LEAVES

→LOOK FOR THIS
Keep an eye out for "witches' brooms" on **COMMON HACKBERRY** branches. These are twisted clumps of twigs that grow where the trees have been attacked by little insects or by fungi, which causes them to become misshapen. The twigs are odd looking but harmless. And look for its natural but unusual bark with corky-looking lumps. Some call it "warty."

American Elm

Ulmus americana HEIGHT 60–100 ft (18.5–30.5 m) · SHAPE Medium size to tall, straight trunk branching into a V shape, broad crown · LEAVES Alternate, simple, 3–5 in (7.5–12.5 cm), pointed oval, toothed edges · FLOWERS Small, green to red · FRUITS Rounded samaras (wings) · RANGE Southern Canada, eastern and central United States · HABITAT Woods, riverbanks, stream banks · OTHER NAME White Elm

The grand American Elm was once common in woods and parks across much of the United States. People planted them along streets because their stout branches would form a graceful arch across the road. They were long-lived trees that could grow in a wide range of places. However, Dutch elm disease has killed most American Elms. This disease is caused by a fungus carried from tree to tree by beetles. Scientists are now trying to breed American Elms that resist the disease. One day you may see these tall trees along the street again.

BE A TREE HUGGER!

More than a thousand American Elms still stand in New York City's Central Park. They were planted in 1860. Tree scientists work hard to keep Dutch elm disease from spreading to these famous trees.

FRUITS ARE ROUNDED SAMARAS WITH A NOTCH AT THE TIP.

OVAL, POINTED LEAVES WITH TOOTHED EDGES

Slippery Elm

Ulmus rubra HEIGHT **50–80 ft (15–24.5 m)** SHAPE **Medium size; tall, straight trunk; broad crown** LEAVES **Alternate, simple, 5–7 in (12.5–18 cm), pointed oval, toothed edges** FLOWERS **Small reddish clusters** FRUITS **Rounded samaras (wings)** RANGE **Eastern and central United States** HABITAT **Damp woods, hillsides** OTHER NAME **Red Elm**

OVAL, POINTED, TOOTHED LEAVES, ROUGH ON TOP AND HAIRY UNDERNEATH

What's slippery about the Slippery Elm? Its bark! An oily liquid seeps out of the inner bark. For centuries, people have used it in cough syrup and other medicines. The tree's scientific name means "red elm," because the tree has red wood. Dutch elm disease and a disease called elm yellows, which hurts the tree's leaves, have killed off many Slippery Elms.

BE A TREE HUGGER!

Native Americans used to make houses, ropes, and canoes out of Slippery Elm bark.

SHINY, OVAL, POINTED, TOOTHED LEAVES

Rock Elm

Ulmus thomasii HEIGHT **50–100 ft (15–30.5 m)** SHAPE **Medium size to tall; tall, straight trunk; narrow crown** LEAVES **Alternate, simple, 2–4 in (5–10 cm), pointed oval, toothed edges** FLOWERS **Small reddish clusters** FRUITS **Rounded samaras with wings** RANGE **Great Lakes area to Tennessee** HABITAT **Woods, rocky hillsides** OTHER NAME **Cork Elm**

The wood of the Rock Elm is rock-hard. That's why it has been used to make wooden ships, furniture, and hockey sticks. In fact, the wood was so popular for shipbuilding in earlier centuries that most of the trees were cut down. For that reason, you won't see many old, large Rock Elms today. Like the fruit of other elms, the Rock Elm's fruits are carried in round, winged samaras. Rabbits, squirrels, chipmunks, and mice love to eat these seeds when they fall to the ground.

NAME GAME

The Rock Elm's other common name, Cork Elm, describes corky ridges that stick out like dragon scales from the elm's branches.

TREE-MENDOUS: TREES UNDER ATTACK!

CUTTING DOWN TREES FOR COMMERCIAL USE IS CALLED LOGGING. TOO MUCH LOGGING CAN HARM A TREE-HEALTHY ENVIRONMENT.

When left alone, trees usually live in a healthy, balanced way with other plants and animals that are natural to the trees' environment. This balance can change when something breaks up the natural order. People may cut down too many trees or a warming climate may hurt helpful animals. Sometimes people bring in plants or insects from other countries, whether on purpose or by accident. These invaders can kill off unprotected trees unless tree scientists find a way to fight them. Here are just a few of the threats to today's trees. Talk to your local Arbor Day Foundation to find out how you and your friends can help solve tree problems in your community.

Insects

GYPSY MOTHS In the 1860s, an artist named Étienne Trouvelot returned from a trip to France with a collection of gypsy moth eggs. The moths that hatched from these eggs escaped into his Boston neighborhood. By 1900, gypsy moths had spread through the Northeast. Their larvae ate the leaves of trees, such as oaks and aspens, and killed many within a few years. This continues today. In the early 1990s, watchful experts stopped a new kind of gypsy moth from entering the United States by quickly destroying it as it came off a ship.

MOUNTAIN PINE BEETLES These tiny bark beetles are native to the West. They weren't a big problem and remained contained in certain areas until the 1990s, when warmer, drier weather led them to spread through pine forests. They lay their eggs in the wood under the bark, and over time this kills the trees. The beetles have destroyed millions of pines in the western states.

Plants and Fungi

OAK WILT Like many tree diseases, oak wilt is caused by a fungus. Fungi (the plural of fungus) are neither plants nor animals. They are organisms, such as mushrooms or molds, that live off of other things, living or dead. The oak wilt fungus gets into oak wood and cuts off the flow of water in the tree. It is helped along by beetles, which carry the fungus's spores (tiny seeds) from tree to tree. The oaks turn brown and die off. Many oaks in the central United States are dying from oak wilt.

KUDZU The vine known as kudzu was brought to the United States from Asia in 1876. It was sold as a plant that would help keep loose soil from washing away. In its new home, the vine spreads like wildfire. It swarms up tree trunks and covers tree branches, growing up to one foot (30.5 cm) per day. The thick blanket of leaves cuts off light to the trees beneath it. Kudzu grows so fast that it is sometimes called the "vine that ate the South." In some very moist places, you can hold a ruler next to a kudzu vine and see it grow!

White Ash

Fraxinus americana HEIGHT **70–100 ft (21.5–30.5 m)** · SHAPE **Medium size to tall; tall, straight trunk; dense crown** · LEAVES **Opposite, compound, 8–12 in (20.5–30.5 cm), 5–9 leaflets** · FLOWERS **Green to purplish clusters** · FRUITS **Samaras (wings)** · RANGE **Eastern United States** · HABITAT **Moist slopes, woods; streets and parks** · OTHER NAME **Biltmore Ash**

A graceful tree with bright leaves in autumn, the White Ash is often planted along streets and in yards. Its strong wood is valuable and useful, particularly for baseball bats. Deer and rabbits eat the tree's bark. Many kinds of birds, squirrels, and mice make a meal of the samaras (the winged seeds). An insect called the emerald ash borer is now killing White Ashes by the millions. This shiny beetle was brought into the United States from Asia in 2002. Its larvae eat into the tree's wood and can kill an ash in a couple of years. Tree scientists are trying to find ways to stop them.

→LOOK FOR THIS
The ridges in **WHITE ASH** and **GREEN ASH** bark make a diamond pattern.

FIVE TO NINE LEAFLETS ON COMPOUND LEAVES; GREEN ON TOP, PALE TO WHITISH UNDERNEATH

FRUITS ARE SAMARAS IN CLUSTERS.

Green Ash

Fraxinus pennsylvanica HEIGHT **60–70 ft (18.5–21.5 m)** · SHAPE **Medium size; tall, straight trunk; irregular crown** · LEAVES **Opposite, compound, 6–10 in (15–25.5 cm), 7–9 leaflets** · FLOWERS **Purplish clusters** · FRUITS **Samaras** · RANGE **Eastern and central United States** · HABITAT **Damp forests, stream banks; streets and parks** · OTHER NAMES **Red Ash, Swamp Ash**

The Green Ash is found all over the United States east of the Rockies and north into Canada. It grows fast and can live in hot or cold places. It's a little smaller than the White Ash, but like that tree it is slender and straight. People often plant Green Ashes in yards, parks, and along streets. Like the White Ash, the Green Ash can be killed by the pesky emerald ash borer.

FIVE TO NINE LEAFLETS ON COMPOUND LEAVES; GREEN ON TOP, LIGHT GREEN UNDERNEATH

EXPERT'S CIRCLE

DON'T BE FOOLED White and Green Ashes look alike. To tell which is which, check out the leaves. White Ash leaves are very pale, almost white, on the bottom. Green Ash leaves are light green on their undersides.

UPRIGHT YELLOW FLOWER CLUSTERS

Ohio Buckeye

Aesculus glabra HEIGHT **30–50 ft (9–15 m)** · SHAPE **Small to medium size, straight trunk, broad crown** · LEAVES **Opposite, compound, 2–6 in (5–15 cm), 5–11 leaflets** · FLOWERS **Yellow clusters** · FRUITS **Prickly capsules** · RANGE **Eastern and central United States** · HABITAT **Damp slopes, riverbanks, stream banks** · OTHER NAMES **Fetid Buckeye, American Horse-Chestnut**

The Ohio Buckeye has its good qualities and bad qualities. The tree has a nice shape and pretty, upright flower clusters in spring. Its spiky fruits split open to show a shiny brown seed. With its pale scar down the middle, the nut looks like a deer's eye, or buckeye. However, the tree is given another name—Fetid Buckeye—for a good reason. "Fetid" means "stinky," and the Ohio Buckeye's leaves, twigs, bark, and flowers all smell nasty when they are crushed.

COMPOUND LEAVES WITH 5 TO 11 LEAFLETS FANNING OUT FROM CENTRAL POINT

DANGER!

The Ohio Buckeye isn't just stinky—it's poisonous! Never eat any part of the tree, including its seeds.

Common Sumac

Rhus glabra HEIGHT 10–25 ft (3–7.5 m) · SHAPE Small, sometimes shrublike, one or many trunks, broad crown · LEAVES Alternate, compound, 12–18 in (30.5–45.5 cm), 7–31 leaflets · FLOWERS White clusters · FRUITS Red berrylike clusters · RANGE Across the United States, mainly in the East · HABITAT Fields, roadsides · OTHER NAME Smooth Sumac

You've seen the Common Sumac, even if you didn't know it. This shrubby tree grows almost everywhere along roadsides and in open areas. Its long compound leaves are bright red in autumn. Its big clusters of fruit are red, too, and feed hundreds of kinds of birds through the winter. The birds spread the seeds in their droppings, helping the tree spring up in new spots.

10s spotters

LONG, COMPOUND, TOOTHED LEAVES

LARGE CLUSTERS OF RED FRUIT

EXPERT'S CIRCLE

DON'T BE FOOLED

Common Sumac won't give you a rash, but its relative Poison Sumac will. Unlike Common Sumac, Poison Sumac grows only in the East in wet, swampy areas. Its leaves are smaller, with fewer leaflets. Don't touch if you're not sure which one is which.

Mimosa

Albizia julibrissin HEIGHT **20–50 ft (6–15 m)** SHAPE **Small, sometimes shrublike, one or many trunks, round crown** LEAVES **Alternate, compound, 6–15 in (15–38 cm), 3–12 leaflets in pairs** FLOWERS **Pink clusters** FRUITS **Flat pods** RANGE **Native to Asia; New York to California** HABITAT **Roadsides, cleared areas** OTHER NAMES **Silktree, Silky Acacia**

The Mimosa's feathery leaves and fluffy flowers make it a pretty little tree. It was brought to the United States from Asia in the 1700s. Without any natural enemies, the tree spread quickly, and it is now an invasive plant. Its leaves are twice compound: The leaflets themselves have smaller leaflets, which are dark green on top and paler on the bottom. In summer, sweet-smelling flowers that look like pink pom-poms bloom on the ends of its branches.

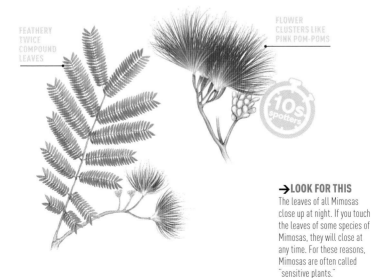

FEATHERY TWICE COMPOUND LEAVES

FLOWER CLUSTERS LIKE PINK POM-POMS

→ **LOOK FOR THIS**
The leaves of all Mimosas close up at night. If you touch the leaves of some species of Mimosas, they will close at any time. For these reasons, Mimosas are often called "sensitive plants."

YELLOW FLOWERS HAVE ONE WHITE PETAL.

TINY COMPOUND LEAVES

Yellow Paloverde

Parkinsonia microphylla HEIGHT 10–25 ft (3–7.5 m) · SHAPE Small, sometimes shrublike, trunk branching into several stems, broad crown · LEAVES Alternate, compound, 1 in (2.5 cm), in pairs · FLOWERS Yellow clusters · FRUITS Hanging pods · RANGE Arizona and California · HABITAT Deserts · OTHER NAME Little-leaf Paloverde

You won't see Yellow Paloverdes in most of the United States, but in the Arizona desert you'll spot them everywhere. They are tough, shrubby trees that can survive in very dry places. Their branches are yellow-green, and their flowers are yellow. In the hottest part of summer, the trees drop their leaves so they won't lose water through the leaves into the air. When the weather cools, the leaves grow back.

DANGER!

Spiny tree alert! The Yellow Paloverde has short, sharp spines where its leaves attach to its branches.

Honeylocust

Gleditsia triacanthos HEIGHT 30–80 ft (9–24.5 m) · SHAPE Medium size; straight trunk; broad, open crown · LEAVES Alternate, compound, 4–14 in (10–35.5 cm) · FLOWERS Greenish clusters · FRUITS Flat pods · RANGE Midwest and south-central United States · HABITAT Woods, fields · OTHER NAMES Thorny Locust, Sweet Locust, Sweet-bean

ONCE OR TWICE COMPOUND LEAVES

The fast-growing Honeylocust tree is known for several things. Its wood is hard and strong, and it is often used in furniture, fence posts, and tools. Its fruit pods hold a sweet pulp that feeds deer, rabbits, farm animals, and other creatures. Huge, sharp thorns grow out of its trunk and branches. These thorns are so big and tough that people have used them as pins and even nails. By experimenting, tree scientists have been able to grow some kinds of Honeylocusts that don't have thorns. Those are the kind that people usually plant along streets and in yards.

DANGER!

Wild Honeylocusts can have sharp thorns up to 12 inches (30.5 cm) long growing from their branches or trunks.

Kentucky Coffeetree

Gymnocladus dioicus HEIGHT 60–100 ft (18.5–30.5 m) · SHAPE Medium size to tall, medium to high trunk branches out, narrow crown · LEAVES Alternate, twice compound, 12–36 in (30.5–91.5 cm) · FLOWERS White in clusters · FRUITS Long pods · RANGE Midwest, south to Louisiana · HABITAT Wooded floodplains · OTHER NAME American Coffee Bean

The Kentucky Coffeetree has big branches, big leaves, and big seedpods. Its leaves are among the largest of any tree: up to three feet (1 m) long, with rows of twice compound leaflets. Early settlers used to roast the seeds to make a kind of coffee. Don't eat the seeds, pods, or leaves, however, because they are poisonous when they aren't roasted.

HUGE TWICE COMPOUND LEAVES

BIG BROWN SEEDPODS

WHITE FLOWERS IN CLUSTERS

NAME GAME

The Kentucky Coffeetree's genus name, *Gymnocladus*, means "naked branch." Its leaves come out late in spring and drop early in fall, so its branches are bare for about half the year.

DANGER!

The leaves, seeds, and pods of this tree are poisonous.

Honey Mesquite

Prosopis glandulosa HEIGHT 20–30 ft (6–9 m)
· SHAPE Small, sometimes shrublike, single trunk or many trunks · LEAVES Alternate, twice compound, 5–10 in (12.5–25.5 cm) · FLOWERS Yellowish in clusters · FRUITS Long pods · RANGE Central Texas to California · HABITAT Deserts, grasslands · OTHER NAMES Glandular Mesquite, Algaroba

Honey Mesquites grow in many shapes and sizes, depending on where they live. Where they have good water and aren't disturbed, they grow into taller, single-trunk trees. In drier places with animals trampling them, they may be small, many-stemmed shrubs. If there is water deep underground, the tree grows a long root downward, about 40 feet (12 m) or more, to reach it. If the only water is near the surface, the tree's roots grow sideways, reaching 60 feet (18.5 m) long or more. Pods that drop from the branches help feed ranch animals, but thorns that also drop are sharp, so step carefully near this tree!

TRY THIS!

HOW DOES WATER MOVE THROUGH PLANTS?

Trees pull water up into their leaves using special tubes called xylem. You can see this happen in this simple experiment. Make sure you have an adult's permission and help. You'll need:

• 3 leaves, each from a different tree, freshly cut with some stalk attached
• 3 clear cups
• Red or blue food coloring

1. Place each leaf into a clear cup and fill the cup about halfway with water.
2. Add enough food coloring to the water to make it pretty dark.
3. Watch the leaves from day to day. Do you see the colored water traveling up the stalk and into the leaf? Through which leaf does water travel fastest?

TWICE COMPOUND LEAVES IN PAIRS

FLOWERS IN NARROW YELLOW CLUSTERS

FRUITS IN LONG, LUMPY PODS

10s spotters

Velvet Mesquite

Prosopis velutina HEIGHT 30–50 ft (9–15 m)
SHAPE Small; sometimes shrublike; short, branching trunk · LEAVES Alternate, twice compound, 3–6 in (7.5–15 cm) · FLOWERS Yellowish in spikes · FRUITS Long pods · RANGE Central and southern Arizona · HABITAT Deserts, dry woods and grasslands · OTHER NAME Mesquite

The Velvet Mesquite is a tough little tree with feathery leaves. Animals love to eat its seedpods, which are full of sugar and healthful proteins. The tree feeds mice, rabbits, squirrels, skunks, coyotes, quail, doves, collared peccaries (a wild piglike animal), and more. Lizards live in the branches and sleep under the tree's bark. Like its relative the Honey Mesquite, the Velvet Mesquite can send deep, deep roots down into the ground to reach water. People often cut it for its dry wood, which burns with a particularly hot flame.

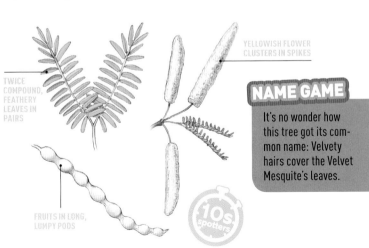

TWICE COMPOUND, FEATHERY LEAVES IN PAIRS

YELLOWISH FLOWER CLUSTERS IN SPIKES

FRUITS IN LONG, LUMPY PODS

NAME GAME

It's no wonder how this tree got its common name: Velvety hairs cover the Velvet Mesquite's leaves.

Black Locust

Robinia pseudoacacia HEIGHT 30–60 ft (9–18.5 m) · SHAPE Medium size, straight trunk, narrow crown · LEAVES Alternate, compound, 8–14 in (20.5–35.5 cm) · FLOWERS Large white clusters · FRUITS Flat pods · RANGE Appalachian Mountains, Ozark Mountains; scattered across the United States · HABITAT Woods, fields; streets · OTHER NAMES False Acacia, Yellow Locust

The Black Locust tree once grew only in the Appalachian and Ozark mountain areas. Today you can find it in most U.S. states. People plant the tree because it has hard, useful wood and sweet-smelling white flowers. New Black Locust trees can spring up from a tree's shallow roots, so it spreads fast wherever it is planted. Now it is turning into an invasive tree, moving beyond its native mountain areas and crowding out other plants.

COMPOUND LEAVES

LARGE WHITE FLOWER CLUSTERS

FRUITS IN FLAT, BROWN PODS

DANGER!

Short, sharp spines stick out of the Black Locust's branchlets.

Black Walnut

Juglans nigra HEIGHT 70–90 ft (21.5–27.5 m)
- SHAPE Medium size to tall, straight trunk, round crown
- LEAVES Alternate, compound, 12–24 in (30.5–61 cm)
- FLOWERS Catkins · FRUITS Large, round, green
- RANGE Eastern United States · HABITAT Damp forests; yards · OTHER NAME Eastern Black Walnut

People value Black Walnut trees for their fine dark wood, which is used to make furniture. Growing all over the eastern United States, these trees can be easily recognized by their large, light-green fruits. Inside the hard fruit husks are tough shells, and inside the shells are tasty nuts. (These are not the same kind of walnuts that you buy in the store.) Squirrels and other creatures will gnaw on the husks until they reach the nuts. It's hard for the average person to get to them without breaking some fingernails and staining their fingers a dark color from the fruit's oils. Recently, Black Walnuts have been hurt by thousand cankers disease, caused by the combined activity of a fungus and the walnut twig beetle.

LARGE
COMPOUND
LEAVES

10s
spotters

SHELL
INSIDE FRUIT
HOLDS NUTS.

FRUIT IS LARGE,
ROUND, AND GREEN.

BE A TREE HUGGER!

Black Walnut trees grow in many yards, but they are not good neighbors. They make a chemical called juglone that can harm many other plants that grow near them.

Bitternut Hickory

Carya cordiformis HEIGHT 70–115 ft (21.5–35 m)
· SHAPE Medium size to tall, straight trunk, round crown ·
LEAVES Alternate, compound, 6–12 in (15–30.5 cm)
· FLOWERS Catkins · FRUITS Greenish nut · RANGE
Eastern United States · HABITAT Stream banks,
swamps, valleys · OTHER NAME Swamp Hickory

You can recognize a Bitternut
Hickory by the large leaflets
on its compound leaves and by
the greenish husks of its nuts.
In winter, the buds at the ends of
its branches turn bright yellow. This
tall tree grows throughout the eastern
United States, particularly in places with wet
soils. It is sometimes planted as a shade tree for
streets and yards. Its wood, hard and long-lasting,
is used to make furniture and tool handles.

COMPOUND LEAVES
WITH 7 TO 11 LARGE
LEAFLETS

10s
spotters

NUTS INSIDE
GREENISH HUSKS

NAME GAME

The Bitternut Hickory
is well named. Its nuts
are so bitter that not
even squirrels will
eat them.

Pignut Hickory

Carya glabra HEIGHT **50–80 ft (15–24.5 m)**
· SHAPE **Medium size, straight trunk, irregular crown**
· LEAVES **Alternate, compound, 8–10 in (20.5–25.5 cm)** · FLOWERS **Catkins** · FRUITS **Brown nut** · RANGE **Eastern United States** · HABITAT **Woods, ridges** · OTHER NAMES **Smoothbark Hickory, Broom Hickory**

These slow-growing trees with short, drooping branches are common in the hills of the eastern United States. Most are of medium size, but older ones can be more than a hundred feet (30.5 m) tall. Their oval or pear-shaped nuts, which contain a lot of fat, are a big part of the diet of many animals. Squirrels, turkeys, black bears, raccoons, foxes, and chipmunks all feed on them.

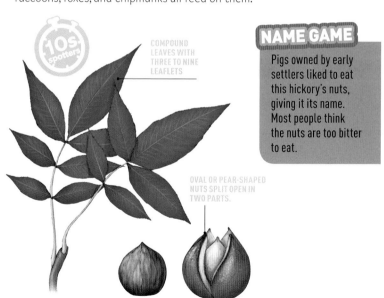

COMPOUND LEAVES WITH THREE TO NINE LEAFLETS

OVAL OR PEAR-SHAPED NUTS SPLIT OPEN IN TWO PARTS.

NAME GAME

Pigs owned by early settlers liked to eat this hickory's nuts, giving it its name. Most people think the nuts are too bitter to eat.

Pecan

Carya illinoinensis HEIGHT 70–100 ft (21.5–30.5 m)
· SHAPE Tall, straight trunk, rounded crown · LEAVES
Alternate, compound, 12–20 in (30.5–51 cm) · FLOWERS
Catkins · FRUITS Brown nut · RANGE Southern and central
United States · HABITAT River valleys, low areas · OTHER
NAMES Sweet Pecan, Hardy Pecan

The Pecan is a tall tree with a big trunk that spreads out into heavy branches. It grows best in warm river valleys, particularly around the Mississippi River. However, it is widely planted in yards and on farms for one tasty reason: its nuts. Starting when the tree is around eight years old, it produces two-inch (5-cm) fruits with a thin husk. When the husk cracks open in four pieces in the autumn, it reveals the pecan nut, its seed. Pecans are widely used in cookies, salads, pies, and other delicious dishes.

Laugh Out Loud!

Knock, knock.

Who's there?

Pecan.

Pecan who?

Pecan somebody your own size!

COMPOUND LEAVES
WITH 9 TO 17 LEAFLETS

OVAL NUTS IN
THIN HUSKS

HUSKS OPEN
IN AUTUMN
TO REVEAL
A SEED.

Big Shellbark Hickory

Carya laciniosa HEIGHT 60–100 ft (18.5–30.5 m) · SHAPE Tall, straight trunk, cylinder-shaped crown · LEAVES Alternate, compound, 12–24 in (30.5–61 cm) · FLOWERS Catkins · FRUITS Large nut · RANGE Eastern and central United States · HABITAT River valleys, stream banks · OTHER NAMES Shellbark Hickory, King Nut Hickory, Bottom Shellbark

COMPOUND LEAVES USUALLY HAVE SEVEN LEAFLETS.

Tall and slow growing, the Big Shellbark Hickory likes wet areas such as river valleys. You can recognize it by its big hickory nuts, just smaller than tennis balls—the largest nuts of any hickory tree. Its bark peels up in flat strips, and its twigs are orange. Strong, flexible Big Shellbark Hickory wood is prized for furniture and cabinets. Animals and people alike enjoy eating hickory nuts.

BE A TREE HUGGER!

Before he became president, Andrew Jackson was given the nickname "Old Hickory" because of his toughness in battle.

Shagbark Hickory

Carya ovata HEIGHT 70–100 ft (21.5–30.5 m) · SHAPE Tall, straight trunk, irregular crown · LEAVES Alternate, compound, 8–14 in (20.5–35.5 cm) · FLOWERS Catkins · FRUITS Round nut · RANGE Eastern and central United States · HABITAT River valleys, hillsides · OTHER NAMES None

COMPOUND LEAVES USUALLY HAVE FIVE LEAFLETS.

Shagbark Hickories bear round, sweet nuts that are said to be the tastiest of all the hickories because of their distinctive flavor and texture. The trees are called Shagbark for good reason. Although young trees have smooth gray bark, older trees have very shaggy bark that peels up in thick, curling strips. Shagbark Hickory wood is strong and heavy. It's good for making tools and to use for firewood.

EXPERT'S CIRCLE

DON'T BE FOOLED You can tell Big Shellbark (top) and Shagbark Hickories apart by their leaves. Big Shellbark leaves usually have seven leaflets without hairs at the tips. Shagbark leaves usually have five leaflets and hairs at the tooth tips. Their bark is also different: A mature Shagbark has thicker curling strips than a Big Shellbark does.

Shagbark Hickory   Big Shellbark

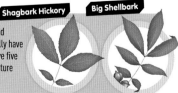

Mockernut Hickory

Carya tomentosa HEIGHT 60–80 ft (18.5–24.5 m) · SHAPE Medium size, straight trunk, rounded crown · LEAVES Alternate, compound, 9–14 in (23–35.5 cm) · FLOWERS Catkins · FRUITS Round nut · RANGE Eastern and central United States · HABITAT Hillside and ridges · OTHER NAMES None

FIVE TO NINE LEAFLETS ON COMPOUND LEAVES; HAIRY ON THE BOTTOM

NAME GAME

Why is it called Mockernut? Because the tree is mocking you: You've spent all that time opening a tough husk just to find a tiny nut.

Like other hickories, the Mockernut is a straight, slow-growing tree with strong wood. Unlike the Big Shellbark or Shagbark (see page 139 for both), its bark has ridges, but it never peels off in strips. The compound leaves have a hairy, velvety underside. The tree's nuts are held inside a heavy, thick husk. Squirrels, rabbits, and bears will happily break open the husks to get at the sweet little nuts. People usually find that the nut is not worth the effort it takes to crack open the husk that holds it.

Tree of Heaven

Ailanthus altissima HEIGHT 40–70 ft (12–21.5 m) · SHAPE Medium size, straight trunk, irregular crown · LEAVES Alternate, compound, 12–36 in (30.5–91.5 cm) · FLOWERS Yellow-green clusters · FRUITS Samaras in clusters · RANGE Native to China; throughout United States · HABITAT Woods, river valleys; roadsides, city streets · OTHER NAMES Ailanthus, Paradise Tree

VERY LONG COMPOUND LEAVES

The Tree of Heaven is native to China, but it was brought to the United States in the 1700s. It turned out to be far from heavenly. Its huge leaves smell like rotting nuts. It grows very quickly, adding up to six feet (2 m) in height per year. It spreads quickly, too, through its flying seeds and by sprouting new trees from its roots. Before long, one tree will turn into a thick mass of trees. Like the Black Walnut (see page 135), the Tree of Heaven makes a chemical that slows down or kills the plants around it. Now this tree has invaded many parts of the United States, from cities to forests, choking out native plants.

Chinaberry Tree

Melia azedarach HEIGHT 30–50 ft (9–15 m) · SHAPE Small, straight trunk, rounded crown · LEAVES Alternate, twice compound, 12–24 in (30.5–61 cm) · FLOWERS Pale purple in clusters · FRUITS Small, yellowish, berrylike · RANGE Native to Asia; southern United States · HABITAT Roadsides, open fields · OTHER NAMES Pride of India, Bead-tree

A French tree scientist brought the first Chinaberries to the United States in the 1700s. People liked them because they had sweet-smelling purple flowers and beautiful wood. People could also make necklaces out of the dried fruits, which look like beads. However, like many non-native plants, the Chinaberry turned out to be a weed. It spreads quickly in disturbed areas, like roadsides. Its fruit is highly poisonous, but its leaves are useful as a natural insect repellent. Some people plant Chinaberries around their home to provide shade and repel mosquitoes.

LARGE, TWICE COMPOUND LEAVES

PURPLE FIVE-PETALED FLOWERS IN CLUSTERS

SMALL BERRYLIKE FRUIT

DANGER!
The Chinaberry's little fruits are poisonous. Do not eat them, and keep them away from pets, too.

Joshua Tree

Yucca brevifolia HEIGHT 15–40 ft (4.5–12 m) · SHAPE Small; short, thick trunk; broad crown · LEAVES Sword-shaped, in clusters, 6–14 in (15–35.5 cm) · FLOWERS Whitish in large clusters · FRUITS Capsules · RANGE Mojave Desert, Southwest United States · HABITAT Deserts · OTHER NAME Yucca Palm

With its armlike branches that end in clusters of spiky leaves, the Joshua Tree looks like a tree from another planet. These trees are native to the Mojave Desert. (In fact, a national park in California is named after them.) Young Joshua Trees may just have a straight trunk and no branches. The branches grow only after the tree has bloomed for the first time. Old leaves stay on the trees, forming a kind of shaggy covering. Scientists aren't sure how old these trees get because the trunks don't have rings they can count. They think the oldest ones have lived 150 years or more.

BE A TREE HUGGER!

Only one insect, the yucca moth, carries pollen between Joshua Trees. Without the yucca moth, the trees would die out.

SHARP, STIFF, SWORDLIKE LEAVES IN CLUSTERS

FLOWER CLUSTERS UPRIGHT AT TIPS OF BRANCHES

DANGER!

Watch out! Joshua Tree leaves are tipped with sharp, sharp spines.

Cuban Royal Palm

GIANT COMPOUND LEAVES WITH SLENDER LEAFLETS

Roystonea regia HEIGHT **70–100 ft (21.5–30.5 m)** · SHAPE **Medium size to tall, tall trunk, crown of drooping fronds** · LEAVES **Huge, compound, 9–13 ft (3–4 m)** · FLOWERS **Long white clusters** · FRUITS **Small, red to purple, berrylike** · RANGE **Southern Florida** · HABITAT **Swamps, roadsides** · OTHER NAMES **Royal Palm, Florida Royal Palm**

Cuban Royal Palms are stately trees that line many streets in Florida. Their tall trunks have a gray, ringed surface until close to the top, where they turn green. This green "crownshaft" is actually the base of the leaves, which curve out in a drooping crown. Each palm leaf is huge—up to 13 feet (4 m) long—and covered with long, dangling leaflets. Cuban Royal Palms grow well in the salt air near the sea, but they are disappearing from the wild.

BE A TREE HUGGER!

Bats like to eat the palm's fruit. They spread the seeds in their droppings.

Cabbage Palmetto

Sabal palmetto HEIGHT **30–65 ft (9–20 m)** · SHAPE **Small to medium size, straight trunk, round crown** · LEAVES **Big, compound, fan-shaped, 5–6 ft (1.5–2 m)** · FLOWERS **Long white clusters** · FRUITS **Black, berrylike** · RANGE **North Carolina to Florida** · HABITAT **Marshes, sandy coasts; roadsides and parks** · OTHER NAMES **Cabbage Palm, Palmetto, Sabal Palm**

Cabbage Palmettos grow along the warm and wet coasts of Florida and the Southeast. They have stout, straight trunks without branches, topped by a round crown of big, fan-shaped leaves. On young trees, the trunk is covered by the rough bases of old leaves. In older trees, the trunk has smoothed out. Native Americans put the trees to many uses. They made the trunks into poles for their houses and formed roofs from the overlapping leaves. Dried in the sun, the leaflets can also be woven into baskets.

LARGE, WIDE, FAN-SHAPED COMPOUND LEAVES

NAME GAME

People used to cut off the bud at the top of the Cabbage Palmetto, where new leaves grow. They would eat it, raw or cooked, because it was known to taste like cabbage. However, this kills the tree, so no one does this anymore.

Key Thatch Palm

Leucothrinax morrisii HEIGHT **20–40 ft (6–12 m)** · SHAPE **Small, straight trunk, round crown** · LEAVES **Big, compound, fan-shaped, 2–3 ft (0.5–1 m)** · FLOWERS **Long white clusters** · FRUITS **White, berrylike** · RANGE **Southern Florida** · HABITAT **Marshes, pinewoods; yards** · OTHER NAMES **Brittle Thatch Palm, Sea Thatch Palm**

The Key Thatch Palm is native to far southern Florida, but people in other parts of the state like to plant it in yards and parks. It's a handsome little tree with huge, fan-shaped leaves. Green on top, the leaves are silvery on their undersides. Their tough leaflets can be woven into mats or bundled into brooms.

WHITE FRUITS IN DANGLING CLUSTERS

LARGE, WIDE, FAN-SHAPED COMPOUND LEAVES

10s spotters

EXPERT'S CIRCLE

DON'T BE FOOLED Palm trees don't have separate wood and bark like other trees. Their trunks are one solid mass of plant fibers.

California Fan Palm

Washingtonia filifera HEIGHT 30–50 ft (9–15 m)
· SHAPE Small to medium size, straight trunk, round
crown · LEAVES Big, compound, fan-shaped, 3–6 ft
(1–2 m) · FLOWERS Very long white clusters · FRUITS
Black, in clusters · RANGE Southern Arizona and
Southern California · HABITAT Deserts, stream
banks · OTHER NAMES California Washingtonia,
California Fan Palm, Desert Palm, Petticoat Palm

The California Fan Palm
grows naturally in desert
oases, where there are natural watering holes. However,
people also plant it along
streets and in parks. The tree has
a spiky crown of fan-shaped leaves.
As the leaves die, they droop down and
form a thick skirt around the tree trunk. Many
kinds of animals and insects take shelter in this skirt, including
hooded orioles, western yellow bats, and rat snakes. People who plant
this tree often cut off the skirt so it won't attract insects or rodents.
The tree also grows huge, 10-foot (3-m)-long flower clusters, which
hang from the base of the leaves.

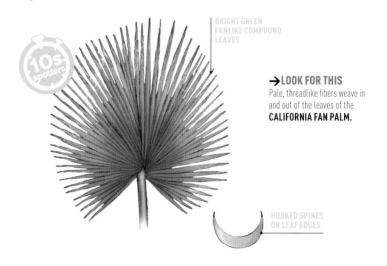

BRIGHT GREEN
FANLIKE COMPOUND
LEAVES

10s
spotters

→ **LOOK FOR THIS**
Pale, threadlike fibers weave in
and out of the leaves of the
CALIFORNIA FAN PALM.

HOOKED SPINES
ON LEAF EDGES

MISSISSIPPI	**Magnolia** (genus *Magnolia*)	pages 98–99
MISSOURI	**Flowering Dogwood** (*Cornus florida*)	page 59
MONTANA	**Ponderosa Pine** (*Pinus ponderosa*)	page 44
NEBRASKA	**Eastern Cottonwood** (*Populus deltoides* ssp. *deltoides*)	page 119
NEVADA	**Singleleaf Piñon** (*Pinus monophylla*)	page 43
NEW HAMPSHIRE	**Paper Birch** (*Betula papyrifera*)	page 69
NEW JERSEY	**Northern Red Oak** (*Quercus rubra*)	page 88
NEW MEXICO	**Piñon Pine** (*Pinus edulis*)	page 38
NEW YORK	**Sugar Maple** (*Acer saccharum*)	page 56
NORTH CAROLINA	**Longleaf Pine** (*Pinus palustris*)	page 44
NORTH DAKOTA	**American Elm** (*Ulmus americana*)	page 122
OHIO	**Ohio Buckeye** (*Aesculus glabra*)	page 127
OKLAHOMA	**Eastern Redbud** (*Cercis canadensis*)	page 76
OREGON	**Douglas-fir** (*Pseudotsuga menziesii*)	page 48
PENNSYLVANIA	**Eastern Hemlock** (*Tsuga canadensis*)	page 48
RHODE ISLAND	**Red Maple** (*Acer rubrum*)	page 54
SOUTH CAROLINA	**Cabbage Palmetto** (*Sabal palmetto*)	page 143
SOUTH DAKOTA	**Black Hills Spruce** (*Picea glauca* var. *densata*)	n/a (see also pages 31–35)
TENNESSEE	**Tuliptree** (*Liriodendron tulipifera*)	page 97
TEXAS	**Pecan** (*Carya illinoinensis*)	page 138
UTAH	**Blue Spruce** (*Picea pungens*)	page 33
VERMONT	**Sugar Maple** (*Acer saccharum*)	page 56
VIRGINIA	**Flowering Dogwood** (*Cornus florida*)	page 59
WASHINGTON	**Western Hemlock** (*Tsuga heterophylla*)	n/a (see also page 48)
WEST VIRGINIA	**Sugar Maple** (*Acer saccharum*)	page 56
WISCONSIN	**Sugar Maple** (*Acer saccharum*)	page 56
WYOMING	**Plains Cottonwood** (*Populus deltoides* ssp. *monilifera*)	page 119

n/a: not listed in this book; in some cases, similar trees are listed after "see also"

Quick ID Guide

CALLING ALL TREE HUGGERS!

Trees are all around you, whether you're in your backyard or on a family vacation to a national park. These profiles will help you quickly identify some that are familiar and some that aren't. Check out their full information on the pages listed with them.

Alaska Cedar - 18
Cypress (Cupressaceae)

Redwood - 20
Cypress (Cupressaceae)

Pacific Silver Fir - 26
Pine (Pinaceae)

Red Spruce - 34
Pine (Pinaceae)

Pacific Yew - 49
Yew (Taxaceae)

Bigleaf Maple - 52
Maple (Aceraceae)

Southern Catalpa - 58
Bignonia (Bignoniaceae)

Flowering Dogwood - 59
Dogwood (Cornaceae)

Empress Tree - 60
Figwort (Scrophulariaceae)

Red Mangrove - 61
Mangrove (Rhizophoraceae)

Pawpaw - 62
Custard Apple (Annonaceae)

American Holly - 63
Holly (Aquifoliaceae)

Red Alder - 64
Birch (Betulaceae)

Yellow Birch - 67
Birch (Betulaceae)

Common Persimmon - 73
Persimmon (Ebenaceae)

Sourwood - 74
Heath (Ericaceae)

Crape Myrtle - 75
Loosestrife (Lythraceae)

Eastern Redbud - 76
Pea (Fabaceae)

American Beech - 76
Beech (Fagaceae)

White Oak - 78
Beech (Fagaceae)

Witch Hazel - 94
Witch Hazel (Hamamelidaceae)

Sweetgum - 95
Sweetgum (Altingiaceae)

California Laurel - 97
Laurel (Lauraceae)

Southern Magnolia - 98
Magnolia (Magnoliaceae)

White Mulberry - 101
Mulberry (Moraceae)

Tasmanian Bluegum - 102
Myrtle (Myrtaceae)

Blackgum - 103
Sour Gum (Nyssaceae)

American Sycamore - 104
Plane Tree (Platanaceae)

Sweet Crabapple - 111
Rose (Rosaceae)

Weeping Willow - 117
Willow (Salicaceae)

Quaking Aspen - 120
Willow (Salicaceae)

American Basswood - 121
Linden (Tiliaceae)

American Elm - 122
Elm (Ulmaceae)

White Ash - 126
Olive (Oleaceae)

Ohio Buckeye - 127
Soapberry (Sapindaceae)

Common Sumac - 128
Sumac (Anacardiaceae)

Mimosa - 129
Pea (Fabaceae)

Black Walnut - 135
Walnut (Juglandaceae)

Bitternut Hickory - 136
Walnut (Juglandaceae)

Tree of Heaven - 140
Quassia (Simaroubaceae)

Chinaberry Tree - 141
Mahogany (Meliaceae)

Joshua Tree - 142
Asparagus (Asparagaceae)

Cuban Royal Palm - 143
Palm (Arecaceae)

Glossary

ACHENE: A small, dry fruit with one seed inside

ALTERNATE LEAVES: Leaves arranged on one side of a branch or twig and then the other—not opposite

BARK: The tough outer covering of a tree

BRACT: A little leaf growing from the base of a flower or out of a cone

BRANCH: A large side shoot growing out of a tree trunk

BRANCHLET: A small branch growing out of a larger branch

BROADLEAF: A tree with flat, thin leaves that usually drop in the autumn

CATKIN: A narrow clump of tiny flowers that grows along a stalk

CHLOROPHYLL: A green chemical in plants that helps them make food

CLUSTER: A group of flowers growing together

COMMON NAME: The non-Latin name that most people use, such as Red Oak

COMPOUND: Many small leaflets sticking out of a central stalk

CONE: A mass of overlapping scales that holds a conifer's seeds or pollen

CONIFER: A tree that has cones and, usually, needlelike leaves

CROWN: The spreading top part of a tree made up of branches and leaves

DECIDUOUS: Dropping leaves regularly (usually once a year)

EVERGREEN: Having leaves that stay green throughout the year

FLOWER: A part of a tree or other plant that helps it to reproduce

FRUIT: The part of a flowering tree that holds its seeds

FUNGUS: A plantlike organism, such as a mushroom, that doesn't have chlorophyll

GENUS: A group of related species and the first part of a scientific name, which is in Latin

HABITAT: The place where a plant or animal normally lives

HYBRID: A mix of two different kinds of plants or animals

INVASIVE: Something that spreads, such as non-native plants spreading into native areas

LEAF: The part of a plant, usually green and either flat or needlelike, that makes its food

LOBE: A divided part of a leaf

MIDRIB: The central vein of a leaf

NEEDLE: A thin, pointy leaf found on a conifer

NUT: A dry, hard-shelled fruit

OLD-GROWTH FOREST: A forest having large, old trees

OPPOSITE LEAVES: Leaves arranged right across from one another on a branch or twig

PIONEER: Young plants that are the first to grow in open areas

POLLEN: Tiny yellow grains in a flower

RANGE: Where trees are found in places across the nation

SAMARA: The winged fruit of a tree, sometimes called a key

SAP: The watery part of a plant

SCALE: A very short, scaly-looking conifer leaf that wraps tightly around a twig

SCIENTIFIC NAME: The unique name scientists give to every organism—its genus and species in Latin

SEED: The small part of a plant that can produce a new plant

SEEDLING: A very young tree

SHRUB: A woody plant less than 15 feet (4.5 m) tall

SIMPLE LEAF: Single, flat leaf with either smooth or jagged edges

SPECIES: One kind of organism with common features, and the second part of a scientific name, which is in Latin

TOOTH: The jagged edges on the outside of a leaf

TRUNK: The single, main, woody stem of a tree

VEIN: In a leaf, one of the thin ribs that forms the framework

Find Out More

Want to find out even more about trees? Check out these books, websites, apps, and movies. Be sure to ask an adult to help you search the web to find the sites below.

BOOKS

Bernard, Robin. *A Tree for All Seasons*. National Geographic Kids Books, 2001.

Hopkins, H. Joseph. *The Tree Lady: The True Story of How One Tree-Loving Woman Changed a City Forever*. Beach Lane Books, 2013.

Jaspersohn, William. *How the Forest Grew*. Scholastic, 1992.

Lasky, Kathryn. *The Most Beautiful Roof in the World: Exploring the Rainforest Canopy*. HMH Books for Young Readers, 1997.

WEBSITES

Arbor Day Foundation
arborday.org

Discover the Forest
discovertheforest.org

The Life of a Tree
arborday.org/kids/carly/lifeofatree

APPS

MyNature Tree Guide

vTree

MOVIES

A New Perspective on Trees http://video
.nationalgeographic.com/video/olson-trees

Sky Atlantic/David Attenborough: *Kingdom of Plants 3D*

The Secret Lives of Trees http://video.national
geographic.com/video/short-film-showcase
/the-secret-lives-of-trees

National Geographic: *Climbing Redwood Giants*

Credits

Copyright © 2017 National Geographic Partners, LLC

Published by National Geographic Partners, LLC All rights reserved. Reproduction of the whole or any part of the contents without written permission from the publisher is prohibited.

Since 1888, the National Geographic Society has funded more than 12,000 research, exploration, and preservation projects around the world. The Society receives funds from National Geographic Partners LLC, funded in part by your purchase. A portion of the proceeds from this book supports this vital work. To learn more, visit natgeo.com/info.

NATIONAL GEOGRAPHIC and Yellow Border Design are trademarks of the National Geographic Society, used under license.

For more information, visit nationalgeographic.com, call 1-800-647-5463, or write to the following address:

National Geographic Partners
1145 17th Street N.W.
Washington, D.C. 20036-4688 U.S.A.

Visit us online at
nationalgeographic.com/books

For librarians and teachers:
ngchildrensbooks.org

More for kids from National Geographic:
kids.nationalgeographic.com

For information about special discounts for bulk purchases, please contact National Geographic Books Special Sales: specialsales@natgeo.org

For rights or permissions inquiries, please contact National Geographic Books Subsidiary Rights: bookrights@natgeo.org

Editorial, Design, and Production by Potomac Global Media, LLC

National Geographic Partners, LLC, and Potomac Global Media, LLC, would like to thank the following members of the project team: Kevin Mulroy, Barbara Brownell Grogan, Matt Propert, Tony Dove, Ginger Woolridge, Jane Sunderland, and Tim Griffin.

Designed by Carol Farrar Norton

Library of Congress Cataloging-in-Publication Data
Names: Daniels, Patricia, 1955-
Title: Trees / by Patricia Daniels.
Description: Washington, D.C. : National
    Geographic Kids, 2017. | Series: Ultimate
    explorer's field guide | Audience: Age 9-12. |
    Audience: Grade 4 to 6. | Includes index
Identifiers: LCCN 2017010526 |
    ISBN 9781426328916 (pbk. : alk. paper) |
    ISBN 9781426328923 (hardcover : alk. paper)
Subjects: LCSH: Trees--United States--
    Identification--Juvenile literature.
Classification: LCC QK475.8 .D36 2017 | DDC
    582.160973--dc23
LC record available at https://lccn.loc
    .gov/2017010526

Printed in China
17/RRDS/1